SECURITY

FOR SMALL COMPUTER SYSTEMS

A PRACTICAL GUIDE FOR USERS

Published by

ELSEVIER ADVANCED TECHNOLOGY PUBLICATIONS

on behalf of

COMPUTER SCIENCES COMPANY LTD

In association with

CONTINUITY PLANNING ASSOCIATES BV - NETHERLANDS
CRYPTECH NV - BELGIUM
INFORMATION DYNAMICS - FRANCE

Printed and bound in Great Britain by
Redwood Burn Limited, Trowbridge, Wiltshire

PG 1918

Security for small computer systems.
1. Computer systems. Security. Management.
658.4 '78

ISBN 0–946395–50–0

PREFACE

Small and medium sized computer systems are generally found in office environments and are used directly by the end-users. They may include microcomputers, word processors, Local Area Networks (LANS), small mini-computers or any of these linked to a host mainframe or to national and international networks.

These systems usually cover a limited range of applications. Operating systems are simple and offer only limited possibilities for ensuring security. The end-user is obliged to develop his own security controls and procedures.

In May 1986, a project aimed at producing **practical security advice for non-technical users of smaller systems** began. The project was co-funded by the Commission of the European Communities and a consortium of four European companies:

Computer Sciences Company Ltd	-UK
Continuity Planning Associates BV	-Netherlands
Cryptech NV	-Belgium
Information Dynamics	-France

The project was divided into two phases - fact-finding and reporting. The fact-finding phase involved questioning - by interview or by questionnaire - several hundred users, hardware manufacturers, software suppliers and consultancies across Europe. The aim of the exercise was to discover:

* The level of user awareness of security problems and solutions.
* What manufacturers and software suppliers were offering.
* What security threats were being encountered, and how effective safeguards against those threats were.

The report production phase first produced eight working papers - each dealing with a separate aspect of security. Those working papers were then amalgamated and edited to form this final guide:

Security For Small Computer Systems - A Practical Guide for Users.

The four companies involved in the project would like to acknowledge and thank the Commission of the European Communities, in particular DG Xlll, for co-funding the project, and for advice given during the project. The authors to the guide are:

Computer Sciences Company Ltd
Tricia Saddington
Colm Deehan
Fai Kwong

Cryptech NV
Mario Houthooft
Frank Jorissen

Continuity Planning Associates BV
Ron Ginn
Randall March

Information Dynamics
Paul Todd
Ian Wylie

Illustrations by Elsie R. Lennox

CONTENTS

Chapter	Title	Page

CHAPTER 1

THE NEED FOR SECURITY

1.1 INTRODUCTION

This book has been written to help you, the end user of a small computer system, decide whether or not your system is "secure", and if not, what to do about it. Your system may be a stand alone micro-computer or word-processor, a small mini-computer, or any of these connected to a network. You could be using software packages - spread sheets, word-processing, database, accounting etc - or purpose-written software. Whatever you use your system for you have one thing in common with all other computer users - you are storing and processing information. The information may vary in value, but even the most trivial data has a value (even if only the cost of the time taken to enter it), and will need protecting.

Computer security is time-consuming, slows down processing, aggravates users and can be expensive. So why bother? After all, it will never happen. But "it" does. Over two hundred users of smaller computer systems throughout Europe have given examples of disasters which have happened to their systems. Many, if not all, of these incidents could have been avoided if simple security procedures and controls had been in place.

A micro-computer user, advised to place his data diskettes in a secure place when not in the office, punched holes in the diskettes, rendering them totally useless, and then carefully filed them in a two ring binder. Another user, instructed by security guidelines to take back-up copies of his data files, did - by photocopying the diskettes! He then dutifully filed the resultant, totally useless, sheets of paper securely under lock and key.

Most people simply consider micro-computers, word processors etc. as items of office equipment similar to photocopiers or electric typewriters. That a great deal of information can be stored on small, portable disks, that data media such as diskettes are fairly fragile, that the hardware is portable and that software often contains errors, has not led many people, to date, to take sufficient precautions against threats such as theft, corruption/loss of data, fraud or destruction of the system.

1.2   THE THREAT

What, in practice, does threaten a smaller system? Basically the dangers are similar to those threatening larger mainframe systems. But smaller systems - micro-computers in particular - are not generally placed in special rooms, with entry controls and trained personnel (ie: computer operators) to look after them. Micro-computers pose additional problems in that they are portable. Many families today have micro-computers at home and software and diskettes in use in the office are often compatible with home computers. Data on diskettes is also very portable (200 A4 pages of information can be held on one diskette - the equivalent of a filing cabinet full of data could be carried away in a brief case!).

Threats fall into three major categories - accidental, natural or deliberate. Accidents include fire (which was until recently, the biggest single risk facing most organisations), errors and, for example, maintenance accidents.

In one company on completion of some electrical work, the supply was incorrectly reconnected. This resulted in extensive damage to all of the office automation equipment in a financial institution.

Natural threats include flooding, electric power problems and other environmental hazards.

Deliberate threats include theft, vandalism, terrorism, computer "hacking" and computer related fraud. The danger involved in some of these is reasonably obvious and you can probably judge your degree of exposure without too much difficulty. Others are fairly new, in many cases rapidly growing, and so the exposure may not be so readily appreciated.

Computer "hacking" (unauthorised entry into a system) is often done by people whose motivation is to beat the system. Using a personal computer and a modem to connect it to the telephone system they break into a system and leave some form of message to prove that they have done so. They are becoming more organised, forming into clubs and passing information on how to break into systems to each other via electronic mail "bulletin boards".

International terrorism is another area of growing danger because terrorists are beginning to realise that increasing use of technology, in particular of communication networks, provides new vulnerabilities which they can exploit.

Another increasing threat is computer related fraud. Until recently the greatest exposure to most organisations was fire. Some experts believe that this has changed over the last few years to computer related fraud.

1.3   WHAT IS "SECURITY"?

Computer systems security is not only about protecting the system against intentional acts such as theft, vandalism, fraud - it is also about avoiding the (much more frequent) occurrence of damage from accidents, or minimising the effect of an accident when it does happen.

Most people measure the cost of security against the cost of the hardware and software, and the price of security appears high. However, the cost of security should be weighed against the total value of the system - i.e. the value of the system and data to the organisation. An evaluation often proves that the data is worth several times the value of the hardware and software.

If your computer and data disappeared today, what effect would it have on your business? Could you fall back to a manual system? How long could you manage without the system - a day, a week, a month?

The basic components of good security are control of, and accountability for, access to the computer system and its data.

A small accounts department had been using a stand-alone micro-computer for their day-to-day business - invoicing, sales ledger, general ledger, etc for about six months. They lost the use of the system for a few days (someone spilled a pot of coffee over it), and, having no other computer to fall back on, attempted to revert to their previous manual systems.

This proved impossible - of the three accounts clerks, two had joined since the micro-computer was installed, and the third could not remember, in sufficient detail, what the manual processes were!

A large percentage of computer data loss is attributed to accidental error. By restricting access to systems and data only to those who have a justifiable need, accidentally accessing someone else's data and doing damage can be minimised. Accountability for use of assets (systems, data) is a strong deterrent to any wrong doing.

When implementing security safeguards it is important to maintain a balance between technical controls and administrative procedures. Even the best technical facilities will not be effective if not installed, implemented and maintained with adequate administrative procedures. For example, a card entry access system will not be effective if proper procedures have not been established to control the issue, granting of authority and retrieval of the entry cards.

This diagram illustrates security safe-guards against threats

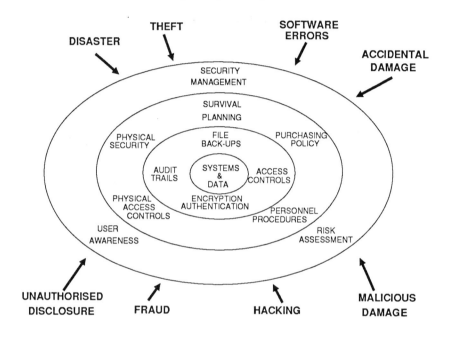

Each of the following chapters considers an aspect of computer security:

Chapters 2 to 5 contains detailed advice on what you should do if faced with threats such as theft, loss of data, fraud etc, while Chapter 6 describes how to decide whether your system is at risk from any of those threats - and what to do about it. Chapter 7, Security Management is oriented towards management of organisational security, and gives guidelines to management on security policy and strategy.

While reading, bear in mind that the basic advice on security is, maintain a sense of proportion and implement the controls and procedures which your system needs.

CHAPTER 2

PHYSICAL SECURITY

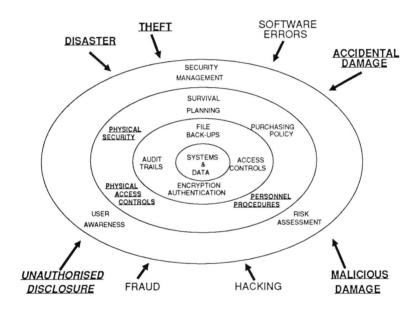

2.1 INTRODUCTION

Computer systems are becoming more portable and accessible. Once they are moved out of the protected environment of the purpose-built computer room into the office or home environment they become more vulnerable.They sit on desks, public counters, beside windows or open doors in view of passers-by, and are left out overnight in unattended offices.

This lays them open to:

*   **THEFT**
*   **DAMAGE** — accidental or deliberate
*   **UNAUTHORISED DISCLOSURE** of information
*   **ENVIRONMENTAL HAZARDS**

2.2   THEFT

In Belgium there was a case of "PC - napping". A small company, who relied on the use of a micro-computer, were held to ransom by someone who stole the whole system (including the data disks). The company paid the ransom.

Is there a history of petty crime in the office? This is a reflection of both the general vulnerability of the office and the attitude of staff and visitors.

Is the office based in an area of high, medium or low crime rates?

How accessible are the system components? Most crime is opportunistic so bear in mind that a busy office may be undisturbed at lunchtime, overnight or at weekends.

What is the value of the components to a potential thief? The key point here concerns the perceived value to the criminal. Modification of a system to reduce its usefulness to others may not prevent theft as the system may still appear to the thief to be a marketable item.

Safeguards

Protect unattended equipment. Do not leave equipment unguarded in an open environment. Offices containing equipment should be locked when not in use, using a lock strong enough to deter casual thieves. Smaller items should be locked away when not in use or outside office-hours. Equipment on public counters can be shielded by security-glass panels or placed behind the counter, or equipment can be securely attached to the counter. (Screwing equipment to desks or walls will discourage the thief). If the screen needs to be viewed from more than one angle then a swivel-screen can be used, allowing the rest of the equipment to be immobilised. Equipment which is not under lock and key should be kept under visual supervision during public hours.

Set alarms. The usual office and home alarm arrangements can be used to detect attempted thefts. Alarms may be placed around the area containing equipment, near-to or on the equipment itself. Doors and windows can be fitted with alarms to detect break-ins. Irrespective of the type of detection system the alarm should always sound in a manned or public area.

Keep inventories and control movements of equipment. Mark all items in clear and ultra-violet with a unique identifier. Item inventories should name the person responsible for custody of that item and a list should be sent out at regular intervals to be signed-off and returned by that person.

Certain items, for example micro-computers or discs holding sensitive information, should not be moved without authorisation. Door-keepers and guards should challenge movement of such items.

Maintain Security Awareness. Encourage staff to challenge movement of restricted items or strangers found on the premises. Keys for cupboards and doors should not be left lying around. Loss of keys should be reported. All staff should be made aware of their security responsibilities and be given the training and resources to be able to meet those responsibilities.

2 . 3   ACCIDENTAL DAMAGE

One of the authors of this book had a PC installed in her city office, two feet from a frequently open window. The office itself is cleaned regularly and thoroughly. After six months the hard disk started giving problems, and quickly became unuseable. All the files on the disk were lost. When the PC was returned to the distributor they found that the hard disk filter was totally clogged up with dust, and the whole of the inside of the machine was dirty. A dust cover put over the machine when not in use solved the problem - and luckily the files on the hard disk had been regularly backed-up (or the first few chapters of this book would have been lost!)

Damage can be caused in many ways. If equipment is moved around it may be mishandled or dropped. Computer systems can also be damaged by food, drink, other liquids, smoke and dust. For example, orange juice spilt on a key-board can glue up the mechanisms causing intermittent faults or making the machine totally unuseable. Dust or smoke in a disc-drive can contaminate the disk surface or heads. Condensation can cause problems if equipment is moved from a cold (eg: air-conditioned) environment to a warmer one. Disk drives are particularly sensitive to this - moisture in the air, condensing on to a hard disk or diskette can cause the drive to fail.

Safeguards

Movement of equipment. If the supplier recommends that he should move the equipment then contact him, if there are instructions for moving the equipment yourself follow these; if there are no instructions then move the equipment with care and, before use, check that all functions are still available. Where possible retain the original packaging boxes for transportation. Before using the equipment after moving it, allow at least one hour for it to adjust to any temperature/humidity changes.

Reduce the likelihood of contamination. Try to avoid eating, drinking or smoking near equipment; store liquids, powders etc. away from equipment. Cover the equipment with dust covers when not in use.

Look after diskettes.

*   Always store in the protective jacket
*   Protect them from being bent
*   Maintain an acceptable temperature range (10-30 degrees C)
*   Use felt tip pen for labelling

2.4   DELIBERATE DAMAGE

A man applying for State Benefits, when told he was not eligible, leapt onto the counter and ran along it kicking in micro-computer screens. The damage done was considerable - not only in repair costs, but also in lost time - the office had to be closed for 24 hours.

First decide whether you might be a target to vandals. Bear in mind the following points:

*   Equipment which is visible to passers-by or visitors will be more vulnerable.
*   Personnel issues can affect the incidence of internal vandalism. Staff see the computer systems as a channel through which to communicate their discontent.
*   Organised or casual vandalism is more likely to occur in certain countries, or areas.
*   Some areas will have higher local crime figures.
*   Multi-national organisations could be a target for particular dissident groups - perhaps because of their "parent" country, or their business area.
*   Government offices may be vandalised by disgruntled members of the public.
*   Organised groups could target companies of whose business they disapprove.
*   Offices may be attached to or near a target.

Safeguards

Vandalism by outsiders. Store data media in fire proof safes or rooms. (If necessary set up bomb resistant safes or rooms.) Limit access to the relevant buildings or offices by minimising the number of entrances, locking and strengthening all windows and other apertures such as air-conditioning vents, pipes and conduits under or between floors.

Set alarms on the periphery or closer to the system components.

Augment or substitute for physical security personnel by CCTV surveillance systems.

(Remember to include all network components in this cover.)

Internal vandalism. Limit access to the computer system to those employees who need to use the equipment.

Lock up equipment or keep it under supervision.

Keep extremely sensitive equipment under internal CCTV surveillance (bearing in mind that problems may be caused if staff find this unacceptable). These safeguards will deter internal vandalism but employees have greater opportunity to cause damage, so consider implementing personnel procedures to minimise dissatisfaction. (See Chapter 4.)

2.5   UNAUTHORISED DISCLOSURE

Information is confidential:

*   **If it should only be available to certain individuals or in limited areas within the company.**
*   **If it should not be released outside the company except under specified circumstances.**
*   **If it falls under national or international privacy legislation (for example, personal data protection laws).**

Companies frequently fail to identify this information when it is stored on small systems, and users who are not aware of the value of the data or of legal obligations cannot be expected to protect the information adequately.

Safeguards

Accidental disclosure. Position screens so that they cannot be overlooked. Ensure that screens are not viewable from public areas. Restrict access to offices which handle confidential information by locks, pass systems or door-keepers. Waste material containing confidential information should be shredded and/or incinerated.

Switch off modems and terminals when not in use so that the lines cannot be used by hackers to read information. (This is particularly important overnight, at weekends and on public holidays.) Control access to all components of networks; including cabling, junction boxes, controllers and concentrators, multiplexors and modems. If these are bugged or modified then eavesdroppers could listen to and possibly record transmissions of confidential information.

Deliberate Disclosure. Keep media holding confidential information under lock and key and only release it to authorised personnel. Install access controls for hardware/software.

2.6   ENVIRONMENTAL HAZARDS

Major disruption can be caused by fires and floods. Fires may originate in the room holding the system or in an adjacent room. Even if the area on fire is small, considerable damage can be caused by smoke contamination.

One organisation suffered a fire in an office containing a mini-computer. Their air-conditioning system carried the smoke through to adjacent offices where several micro-computers were held. As a result, all systems were out of action for over a week.

Water damage can be caused by rain, floods or burst pipes. Pipes are often located in false ceilings or floors, or running along the walls of rooms containing computer equipment. Although the equipment is not often permanently damaged it will be unuseable while equipment and rooms are drying out.

In one company a water pipe burst and flooded a first floor office. No equipment was damaged, but the service of several small computer systems were lost for two days while being dried out.

Power supply defects can cause intermittent corruptions or permanent damage. Power fluctuations can be caused by attaching other electrical equipment to the same power supply as the computer, for example kettles, photocopiers. Disruptions to power supplies can be caused accidentally, for example by cables being drilled through by mistake, or deliberately, by industrial action or sabotage.

A financial institution had a recurring, intermittent problem with the terminals in one office. During the evening, most of the terminals would start behaving erratically, losing data entered or received, or failing completely. Engineers could find nothing wrong with the terminals or the communications equipment.

After several weeks a senior engineer happened to be there when the problem occurred, and heard a noise in an adjacent room. He then discovered that a tumble dryer (doing the Directors' laundry) was plugged into a socket on the other side of the wall from where the terminals were plugged in - on the same ring main. Whenever the tumble dryer was switched on, the terminals went haywire!

Static electricity is another hazard. Small system and network components are sensitive to static at quite low levels: levels of 70 to 300 volts are quoted by manufacturers of anti-static products as being unacceptable. Magnetic fields generated by electric engines can affect electronic equipment.

A journalist found that all the memory on his laptop micro had been wiped clean. This happened three times before he connected it with his journeys on underground train's, and the influence of the magnetic fields from the trains electric motors.

External climatic hazards include earthquakes, lightning storms and high winds. These may damage part or all of the facility, including those areas where system or network components are located. A lightning strike can travel down electric circuits and burnout components.

Near-by radio/radar installations may affect your system because information can be corrupted by the microwave signals from near-by high power transmitters. These need not be obvious or large sources of power, interference can be caused by two-way personal radios.

Recently a computer security consultant was doing a review of security at a financial institution. As he walked towards a "secure" area, the electronically protected door opened - without assistance. He discovered that this was caused by a security guard's hand-held radio telephone - a classic case of one security measure nullifying another.

It is relatively easy to pick up electromagnetic emission from computer equipment, particularly screens. This enables screens to be read from a distance, by fairly inexpensive and portable equipment.

A van, parked in a street near a building occupied by a financial organisation, held equipment capable of detecting and reading data on the micro-computer networks inside the building. The organisation inside the building were totally unaware of the activity until some weeks later when a Director of the company sat down to watch a television programme about computers. Part of the programme was a demonstration of radiation emission detection, and the demonstration showed screens containing his company's data!

Safeguards

Fire. Store data media in fire-proof rooms or safes and minimise the amount of combustible materials held next to or near computer equipment.

If there is a high concentration of systems in one area, then consider automatic controls. They can detect smoke, set off alarms, activate an automatic quenching system, disconnect the power supply and air conditioning, close fire doors (or a selection of these functions.)

Install suitable fire-fighting equipment (automatic or manual); because it is to be used on electrical equipment use chemical suppressants. (Water conducts electricity and could cause damage). Ensure that everybody knows how to use the equipment. Protect the media holding information. Disks, manuals and other portable items can be kept in fire-proof cabinets; remember that these may be inaccessible for some time after a severe fire so back-up copies should be held elsewhere. In order to reduce the risk of electric fires, electrical equipment and supplies must be properly maintained and circuits should not be overloaded.

Switch off equipment overnight. Minimise the amount of waste-paper kept in rooms and have waste-bins emptied at the end of each working day. Discourage or ban smoking.

Floods. The best defence against flooding is to place the system where floods cannot occur. Places to avoid include ground floor and basement areas (which are liable to flooding from rivers, sea or excessive rain) or top floors where the roof may leak and let in rainwater. Note that pipes running above false ceilings or along walls could burst and cause flooding and water damage.

Power Defects. Do not plug computer equipment into the same power point as other equipment. If the system is crucial for your business, set up an alternative power supply in case the regular power supply fails. Generators which will run until power is restored can be obtained. A cheaper solution would be to buy batteries to provide a short-term back-up. If your power supply is erratic install power stabilisers.

If static electricity is a problem, you could install antistatic floor coverings, or antistatic sprays for existing flooring.

Lightning, Earthquake, etc. Unplug equipment from power sockets when not in use or when lightning threatens. Ensure that you have back-up copies of data, and alternative equipment available for use following damage.

Radiation Emission. It is possible to shield equipment - micro-computers, terminals, cabling, etc, but it is still relatively expensive. If, however, a system or network is handling very sensitive data - for example, merger plans - it would be wise to consider shielding it.

Scrambling devices are available, are relatively cheap, and can be effective. Do test these out, in practical conditions, before purchase.

Back up systems. When damage occurs or the system is inaccessible then a contingency facility to support essential work may be necessary. If the system is partially unuseable then duplicate components can be plugged in.

These must be fully compatible so if new versions of equipment or software are installed you may need to buy new spare parts for emergency use. Otherwise arrange for quick purchase and delivery of replacement items.

CHAPTER 3

PROTECTION OF DATA AND SOFTWARE

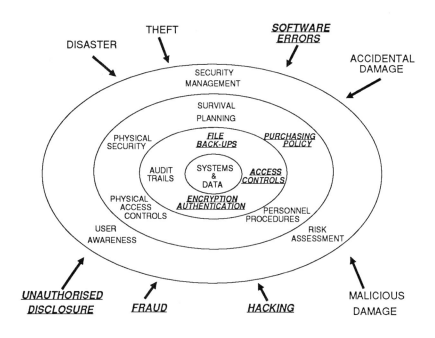

3.1 INTRODUCTION

The value of data held on smaller computer systems and networks is usually underestimated. Yet information is the lifeblood of an organisation, and wrong or missing information can cause anything from temporary inconvenience to major disaster.

In the UK, someone stole a small company's data diskettes and held the company to ransom. They had no secured back-up copies, and could not survive without the data. It included customer mailing lists, orders in progress, and all their accounting information. They paid the ransom demanded.

3.2 THREATS TO DATA AND SOFTWARE

The amount of time, effort, and money expended in protecting any system should, obviously, be in proportion to its value to the company. Ask yourself the following three questions when considering whether or not your computer system needs protection:

* What is the system worth?
* Against whom does it need protection?
* How should it be protected?

What is the system worth? It is not simply the replacement cost of the hardware and software which needs to be considered. It is very often the case that the data stored on the system is worth more than the hardware and software.

In order to assess the value of the data, consider:

How long did it take to enter and store the data? Is it backed-up sufficiently frequently? If not, would it be possible to re-create it?

Is the data financial? If so, is there any way of committing a fraud by manipulating the data (or programs) or otherwise misusing the system? What is the maximum amount that could be obtained by fraud? Consider fraud by stealing one large amount, or many small amounts over a period of time. Who would notice, and when?

Is any of the data personal? If so, is Data Protection legislation in force? What penalties can be exacted if you contravene the law?

Is the data of any possible value to anyone else (inside or outside the organisation)? (For example, new products information, future plans, client information, corporate finance information etc.) Do not forget that even simple mailing lists have a saleable value.

Would any embarrassment, loss of clients/revenue be likely if the data was seen by an unauthorised person? If the unauthorised person changed any of the data could he cause damage to the organisation?

When you have answered these questions fully, you should have a reasonable estimation of the real value of the data to the organisation. This will not necessarily be a precise financial amount but an indication of how important the data is - how much it needs protecting.

Against whom does the system need protection? The answers to this will vary depending on the type of information being held, the organisation and its environment, employee-employer relationships and the current political and industrial situation. Do not ignore the last factor, however unlikely its effect may seem to you - there may be indirect links with more politically sensitive organisations, for example, through shared directors or via customers or suppliers. The following is a useful checklist to assist in answering the question:

* **Insufficiently educated/aware users**
  (data is more often destroyed or corrupted by accident than by design).
* **Other members of staff**
* **Members of the public (if the computer system is in a public area)**
* **Vandals (look at the area in which the building is situated)**
* **Hackers (particularly for systems using public networks)**
* **Thieves - of hardware, software or data.**
* **Terrorists.**

How should the system be protected? If answers to previous questions indicate that the system has no value or has no potential attackers then read no further. This would, however, be a very unusual case and anyone answering so would be advised to seek a second, objective, opinion.

If the answers to the questions suggested that thieves and vandals could threaten the system, then physical protection should be installed - keep offices under lock and key, install burglar alarms etc. (see Chapter 2, Physical Security.)

Safeguards

Classification of Data. Obviously "blanket protection" of all data would be an expensive option - in processing time and in people time. Also, people are reluctant to follow controls and procedures where they feel them to be unnecessary. If security measures are only applied in those areas which are necessary, there is far more likely to be compliance with the measures.

Safeguards to protect data should vary depending on the value of the data. This ensures that at one end of the spectrum there are no costly and time- consuming controls over publicly available data and, at the other end, that highly sensitive confidential data is protected by the most cost effective measures that can currently be implemented.

Before selecting and installing any safeguards, look at the data you use and decide which files are sensitive, confidential or valuable, ie: "classify" your data into one or more levels or classes. It is then possible, for each level, to define the necessary security controls. Highly sensitive data (e.g.future plans) may then be protected by a high level of security, reducing by stages to minimal security for public data (e.g. share prices).

Depending on the amount and sensitivity of your data you could have only two classes of data - that which needs protection and that which needs no protection, or there could be several levels - for example:

Highly sensitive data - access restricted to few, named, personnel.
Medium sensitivity - access restricted to individual sections or departments.
Low sensitivity - no access restrictions.

(A file of information should be classified as the highest classification of data contained within it.)

Classifying the data should result in a clear picture of what data needs protection and what does not - or if you have chosen to use several classifications, to what degree the data needs protecting.

Data Ownership Any data file should be assigned an "owner". Often, in the small system environment the owner is obvious - it is the creator of the file. However, systems are often used by several people and they may all be using the same files. In order to achieve accountability for the reliability and integrity of the data, where there is no obvious owner one should be assigned.

That person should, as well as being responsible for the data, also classify it, and define who should have access to the data. On a micro-computer running only a few applications, perhaps one person could be given overall responsibility and be the "owner" of all files. On a larger system - a mini-computer or net-worked system - there could be several Data Owners, each with responsibility for his own set of files.

Take regular back-up copies. The frequency of taking a back-up copy should vary depending on the rate of change of the data - for example, back-up copies of software should be taken whenever a new version is installed.

Allow programmers access only to development programs - never to programs in "live" production use.

Restrict users from using operating system utilities such as file copying and file deletion programs. (If a user needs such facilities he should be limited to using them only on his own files.)

Restrict access to any software or data file to only those people who need to use it. Store sensitive data on removable hard disks - and lock them away when not in use.

A Manager, in his secretary's absence, needed to refer to a file held on a word-processor. He found the manual, and followed the instructions to attempt to display the file. In the process he managed to delete everyone else's files. Luckily the system had only been in use for a week, or the result could have been disaster. (They had not backed-up any files.)

A word of warning: there are utility programs (e.g. Norton Utilities, Mace Utilities) which allow "back door" access to all information by reading the disc directly. If these utilities, or other similar ones, are available on a system, remove them and then lock them away. Restrict access to only those individuals who need to use them. Any activity while they are being used should be logged - either automatically or manually by a impartial observer.

3.3 ACCESS CONTROLS

A building company collapsed and ceased trading about 18 months after installing a £20,000 micro-based system. A Director of the company claimed that lack of security - in particular access control software - had allowed unauthorised staff to reduce prices, and sell goods at less than cost price. He alleged that this had led to the company's £90,000 a year profit dropping to a £200,000 loss.

You will have noticed that the basic rules for protecting data and software mainly rely on restricting access to the system, software and data. While a certain measure of access restriction can be implemented by manual methods - lock and key, for example, additional restrictions can be imposed by installing and using access control software or hardware. For systems such as mini-computers, access controls may be built in to the operating system. For micro-computers and word processors access controls can be implemented (at additional cost) as, for example, an add-on board.

However an access control system is implemented, it should:

* Identify and verify the user to the system
* Allow each user to access only authorised programs and data. (i.e define his "access rights")
* Log user activities - particularly security violations.
* Allow encryption of data and software.

Identification and verification of user

The system should ensure that the user is an authorised user (identification) and that he or she actually is the person identified (verification). The most widely used method of identification and verification is to enter a User Identification Code (user-id) and a secret Password to the system.

The User-Id is the user's permanent "name" to the system and the user should not be able to change it. It is not usually a secret code, and is often structured depending on department, and position within that department. This in itself introduces a security risk in that most organisations have implemented systems such that the higher within the organisation the user is, the more computer functions he is able to perform. For example:

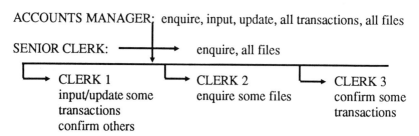

ACCOUNTS MANAGER: enquire, input, update, all transactions, all files

SENIOR CLERK: enquire, all files

CLERK 1
input/update some
transactions
confirm others

CLERK 2
enquire some files

CLERK 3
confirm some
transactions

Typical user-id codes for the above are:-

* **Accounts Manager - ACO1**
* **Senior Clerk - ACO2**
* **Clerks - ACO3, ACO4, etc.**

If you wanted to access this department's files for, for example, fraud, whose user-id would you try to use?

Higher security could be implemented in many companies by not structuring the user-id code so obviously, and not allowing wider access rights automatically to higher levels of personnel.

The password is a secret code, which should be known only to the individual being verified. It has been in use for a considerable time, and is, although widely used, one of the weaker points in the security of systems. The reason for its longevity is that it is still the most cost-effective method of controlling access to computer systems.

The most common password weaknesses encountered are:

* **People forget their password.**
* **They write them down - and many leave them open to view.**
* **They choose obvious passwords - spouse's name, car registration, own name, are among the commonest. (as are "SECRET" and "PASSWORD".)**
* **Passwords are not always encrypted when stored on disk.**
* **Passwords are not changed often enough (if at all).**
* **Password changes are difficult to enforce.**
* **Often users alternate between two passwords.**
* **If password changes are enforced, the user may change on the prescribed day, then revert to their usual password afterwards.**

If a few simple rules are followed, passwords can be an effective security measure:-

* **Keep your password secret and do not write it down.**
* **Do not choose a password with which you can be associated.**
* **Change passwords regularly - at least once a month.**
* **Encrypt passwords while stored on disk.**
* **Delete passwords when no longer required (e.g. after resignation or transfer).**
* **Ensure that passwords are not displayed on screens.**

For a detailed discussion of passwords, password administration, and the weaknesses of passwords, see Annex C, Passwords.

There are other techniques for identifying and verifying users to the system, some of which are becoming widely used for particular types of system and others which are still in the research stage. These are discussed in Annex D - they include smart cards, tokens, and biometric access controls.

User Access Rights

Except for systems which are dedicated to word processing, most small computer systems have a range of software capabilities, for example graphics, database, word processing, spreadsheets, and a range of data files (which are likely to correspond to the software capabilities). Small systems may have a range of authorised users who are entitled to use some (or all) of the software capabilities and some (or all) of the data files. (Most software programs exist on computer systems as files, and can be regarded as data files).

Ideally, when a file is created, the creator or owner of that file should be able to specify which other users may have access to it and what they may do to it, ie: what those other users "access rights" are.

Access Rights should define:

a) the list of programs or data files which a user may access.
b) the types of access allowed - e.g. read, change, create/delete, execute.
c) the method by which the user may access the system -
    (e.g. remote via a network, local, on- line, batch.)

Some access controls packages do allow full definition of access rights, other packages introduce the concept of a System Manager who allocates access to files or directories to individual users.

The latter method of implementation often does not allow the System Manager to limit the type of access - i.e. if a user is given access to a file he may do what he likes with it. It is obviously safer to have facilities to allow full or limited access to files depending on each user's requirement.

Logging of User Activity

Part of the capability of an access control system should be to detect and record breaches in security, e.g. a wrong password entry or an unauthorised attempt to access data. In addition there should be an optional facility to log all activity and identify who has done what.
A security activity log should record the following:

* **Sign-on**
* **Attempted sign-on (e.g. incorrect password)**
* **Sign-off**
* **Forced sign-off (e.g. time-out)**
* **Password change (although the password should not be logged)**
* **Programs and data files accessed**

Other events which may be recorded are system starting and shutdown, and the disabling/enabling of security facilities.

Encryption of Data or Programs

Encryption is the process of transforming information (clear text) into an unintelligible form (ciphertext) so that even if the data is read it is impossible to understand it. The transformation process, or encryption algorithm, is controlled by a "Key". The encryption program uses the key, which is a unique sequence of characters, to encrypt or decrypt any data.

The encryption software (or hardware) is between the user and the data file. An authorised user will enter normal clear text which is then automatically encrypted and stored in unintelligible form. In reverse, when an authorised user wishes to read the data (which he can do only if he inputs the correct "key") it is automatically decrypted before it is presented to him.

When data is encrypted, even if an unauthorised person manages to obtain access to the data he will not understand it (unless, of course, he has also managed to discover how the data was encrypted).

(Annex E contains a more detailed description of encryption.)

3.4   ACCURACY OF SOFTWARE AND DATA

It has long been recognised that the accuracy of software and data is critical in almost all phases of data processing. In most organisations, information produced on large mainframe computer systems and the software used to handle such information has been subject to extensive critical review and error-checking, both during system development and during normal processing.

This has enabled confidence to be placed in the quality of resulting information and other "products" of computer systems.

Smaller computers have made powerful computational and analytical tools available to users throughout many organisations. Increasingly important decisions are being made based on information processed by such systems. Unfortunately, there may be a reluctance to apply the same degree of care (and cost) in integrity assurance as is routinely applied for larger systems. Nevertheless, the formal and official appearance of printed materials which can be produced easily by even micro-computers can result in unwarranted confidence in the substance of such materials.

Where, for example, personal computers are used for routine personal work and are not being used for critical decision-making functions, the lack of formal quality and integrity controls may not be a problem. However, for applications which are critical to the organisation, there should be commensurate quality controls.

Data Accuracy

Even the best software is of little use if it is processing corrupted data. Most generic software tools do not provide built-in facilities for checking the accuracy of input data. Therefore, it becomes the responsibility of you, the user, to build in such checks. These should include data format and range checks and cross-checks of results. Managers should require supporting information and evidence necessary to assure that calculations and other data handling operations have been performed properly.

Software Accuracy

In situations where important functions are being performed on smaller computers, consider applying formal controls over software development and testing.

This does not only apply to situations where systems are being designed and programmed in traditional programming languages (e.g. BASIC). There is increasing use of generic software tools (e.g. spreadsheet and database management systems) to build complex applications. Even though many of the typical programming problems may be reduced in these situations, the need for careful analysis and control is just as important. (This may very well require additional training of personnel or the use of specially trained personnel, since system development skills are not a normal part of professional training).

3.5   PURCHASING SOFTWARE

Allowing uncontrolled purchase of software packages by individuals or departments exposes companies to the following risks:-

* **Difficulties in interfacing packages - i.e. the output data from one package may not be easily input to another if required.**

* **If several different types of computer hardware are being used, then software which runs on one may not run on another.**

* **The supplier may not be sufficiently reliable.**

* **The purchaser may not check the software sufficiently to ensure that it does everything that he needs - now and in the future.**

* **The software may not have sufficient built-in security controls.**

* **The user documentation may be inadequate to run the system efficiently - particularly in the area of errors and recovery from errors.**

* **User help facilities may be absent or inadequate.**

The first two of these cause frustration, annoyance and waste of time (and therefore money). The rest may also have similar effects, but could also cause:

* Errors (in data and software)
* Unauthorised access to the system - which may breach Data Protection Legislation or lay the system open to fraud
* Failure of the system - particularly if it is found, subsequent to purchase, not to perform all required functions.

Implementing a controlled purchasing procedure helps to safeguard against the above - the procedure may be very simple for a small business to fairly complex for a large organisation. A large organisation could survey the market, conduct its own investigation, and produce an approved standard list of products from which internal departments can select those which meet their requirements - a small organisation would have neither the time nor the resources.

If you intend to purchase software ensure that several questions are asked - and responded to satisfactorily. If a supplier's responses are not considered satisfactory another supplier's will be! Prior to talking to suppliers, ask yourself the following two questions:

Have the requirements been fully documented and agreed by all interested parties? "All interested parties" should include the people who are going to be actually using the software. Define all requirements, including:

* Functions to be performed, including monthly and year-end functions;
* Output required - screen, printed, other media;
* Input required and method;
* Ease of use and "user friendliness";
* On-line and off-line help facilities.

How dependent is my business activity going to be (now and in the future) on the software working as specified? If the software - and this particularly applies to small or "one-man" businesses - is likely to become relied on as a major part of the business function, then it is even more important to follow the advice in this section. (It may even be worth paying for a professional consultant to define requirements and assist in evaluating the software packages on the market.)

Once you have answered those two questions, ask the prospective supplier and other users of the software the following:

How reputable and reliable is the supplier? If you do not know the supplier, or have not had previous dealings with them, it is advisable to check up on them. There are several things that can be done:

*   **Check that the company is a member of a professional body and speak to that association's membership secretary.**
*   **Do a company search of the supplier. This will tell you if there have been any changes of name, but, more importantly, will tell you whether the company is making money - see if the turnover complies with what the suppliers may have told you.**
*   **Be wary of salesmen who seem not to know very much about the product they are selling, or the company they work for.**
*   **Seek the advice of your national Computer Society or Association.**

How closely does the software meet your requirements? Your requirements of the software should be documented. Ideally that document should define each requirement as mandatory or optional - and, obviously, all mandatory requirements should be satisfied by the software, and as many of the optional ones as is possible.

Are there other users? If so, who? Any reputable supplier of software will supply you with references of other users. If there is a User Group or Association contact the group and talk to its members about their experience with the system and the supplier.

How adequate is the documentation? Try the documentation out practically - preferably by one of the actual operators of the system using the documentation to operate the system. Check out help facilities, security features and all other functions offered by the package.

What language is the package written in? Beware of packages written in little-known languages: if the supplier does go out of business it will be difficult to get the package maintained - or errors corrected.

What support is offered by the supplier, and at what cost? Support could cover:

* **initial installation**
* **training in use of the software**
* **maintenance and error correction**
* **telephone help-line**

Where possible, check out the quality and effectiveness of the above with existing users.

Does the software have back-up and recovery facilities? All application software packages should have facilities to enable the user to back-up his data (i.e. periodically copy it to another disk or tape).

You, as the potential user of the software, need to decide whether or not recovery procedures are needed. It really depends on how much data is input between each back-up being done. If the system fails, without automatic recovery procedures, you will need to copy the most recent back-up file on to the system and re-do all the operations that have taken place since the last back-up to bring the system up to date again. If this overhead is acceptable, then recovery procedures may not be essential.

What on-line (embedded in the software) help facilities are available? How easy are they to understand and operate? Although a user manual should be available and should answer any queries on the operation of the software, and recovery from errors, an on-line help facility saves operator time (and avoids the frustration of searching through what may be a fairly large manual).

Can the software run on the range of equipment in use in the organisation? This will not always be a requirement - it will depend on the type of organisation, and how the computer systems are used. However, if, for example, a company uses several micro-computers, it improves the efficiency of their use if they can be used to back-up each other.

Can the software interface with other (relevant) packages in use? If so, how? Suppliers will seldom include in their brochures or user manuals, details of how (or whether) their software can communicate with software from other suppliers. It can be a costly and time-consuming operation to get a disk file produced by one software package read and processed by another.

Prior to purchase, spend some time preparing "test data" reflecting the companies day-to-day and ad hoc business, and try out the package. A reputable supplier of reliable software will encourage this. A reputable supplier will also welcome the chance to fully respond to all your questions.

Having purchased and installed the software, store a second copy of the software separately from the system, in a secure place. This will ensure that if the main copy is corrupted - either deliberately, or, as is more usual, accidentally, processing may be restarted using the copy. (Always take a back-up of the back-up before using it!).

It is also well worth ensuring that there is an existing back-up before introducing supplier's updated software versions - until you are certain that the updated software functions correctly.

When you purchase software the supplier will usually not give you the source code - that is, the programs in the language written by the programmer. What you are supplied with, on diskettes normally, is the object code - which is the source code translated into a form understood by the computer system, but non-intelligible to most people (including programmers). If the supplier were to go out of business for any reason, and your software contained errors which did not appear until after that, it would be impossible to get these errors corrected.

A solution to this problem is an "escrow agreement", whereby the source code is deposited with a third party (perhaps a bank, or a solicitor) by the owner of the code. The third party holds the code on terms allowing him to release it to the user (ie: you) in certain circumstances - for example, the bankruptcy or liquidation of the supplier.

3.6 MICRO-COMPUTERS AND WORD PROCESSORS

In the UK, when the personal Data Protection Act became law, one interesting and alarming side-effect occurred. Many computer users who, as required by law, registered their systems, discovered, while they were gathering the information necessary for registration, that there were more micro-computers and word processors in their organisation than had been thought.

They also found that even where there was little or no personal data being held on a system there was quite often a significant amount of sensitive and/or financial data being held on insecure systems. Thus the Data Protection Act did, as a side effect, aid many users by enforcing the production of a total list of systems and data - i.e. assets to be protected.

But less than half of the expected number of users have registered in the UK, and Data Protection legislation has not been enacted in all European countries. There are many organisations, throughout Europe, where there is no central control over the purchase and use of small systems.

The use of various kinds of data is also often not controlled either centrally, or within sections or departments. Often individuals decide what data they are going to hold - and the source from whence it will come.

Without overall control the following are occurring:

* **Out of date or erroneous data is being used for business decisions**
* **User ignorance of data protection legislation results in transgression of the law in some countries**
* **Thefts of data and software**

Safeguards

Out of date or erroneous data. If the same data is being used in more than one system check that it is in phase and preferably comes from a common source.

If the small system is linked to a host computer much of the data is often downloaded from the host. Check that this is done, for all relevant systems, with sufficient frequency (and preferably at the same time). Overnight, for example, may be a good time.

Where data is being input to the system manually, check that there are adequate validation and consistency checks in the software.

Data Protection legislation. For countries where user organisations have a legal obligation to protect personal data, ensure that the end-users are aware of the salient points of the legislation.

Many organisations have produced a small booklet of 4-6 pages, stating the legal position in simple terms, and giving basic advice to personnel to ensure that they adhere to legal requirements. Others include, as part of staff training, some time devoted specifically to data protection requirements. Either, or preferably both, have proved effective, but do need regular re-enforcement.

For personal data, on small systems, it is probable that at least the following safeguards should be in place:-

* Physically controlled access to systems and media
* Access controls (software/hardware) to the system and to the data.
* Encryption of data if it is particularly sensitive.
* Secure disposal of waste media (paper, discs, tapes)
* Secure procedures for transferring output or data media to recipients.
* High end-user awareness of the legal position.

Theft. It is worth briefly reconsidering theft of software and data used in micro-computers and word- processors. Diskettes are very portable, and therefore very easily removed. They are often not filed securely away: in most organisa-tions, of all sizes, they can be seen lying openly on desks, often unsupervised. As an additional attraction to the thief, documentation describing how to use the system is often left conveniently nearby. Micro-computers and word-processors are increasingly becoming compatible with home computers, with a correspond-ing increase in desirability of software found in the office.

Lock away diskettes, removable hard disks and documentation when not in use - particularly when the office is unoccupied. If the micro-computer or word-processor holds particularly sensitive information, also lock the office. Last, but not least, do not forget to take regular back-ups of your files.

Software Piracy (Illegal copying of purchased software). Allowing un-authorised copying of purchased software will render you liable to legal action for infringing the copyright of the software. There is also a risk of purchasing "pirate software" innocently and then receiving no software updates or support because it is pirated.

Always buy software only from authorised dealers.

(Note: pirate software can often be recognised because it is supplied with photocopied documentation - or no documentation at all).

3.7   NETWORKED SYSTEMS

Under this heading, we can include:

* **Networked micro-computers, word-processors and mini-computers**
* **Small machines linked to a host system**

Software or data becomes more vulnerable when in transmission through networks. Whilst it resides in one place physical controls and procedures may more easily be placed on it. It is difficult, if not impossible, to physically secure all paths on a network - unless the network is small and local, and all cables visible. Certainly if using public network facilities you should consider the network as insecure.

The main threat for software or data in transmission is that of unauthorised changes, done by active tapping of the communications lines, or at a network node. (Although theft is also a possibility there are much easier ways to steal software or data than by procuring and using wire-tapping equipment).

It is worthwhile to mention "hackers" as a threat. To date, hackers have tended not to be malevolently inclined, but rather, challenged by a problem. That is, they seek to access systems, unauthorised, and prove that they have done so rather than cause actual damage.

A team of young West German hackers broke into a computer network linking the US space agency NASA with research centres in Europe and Asia. The group broke into the network using relatively cheap home computers and public telephone lines.

If you are using a communications network with dial-in facilities, particularly if it extends outside your immediate environment, be aware of the possibility of access by hackers. It is highly likely that a hacker could inadvertently damage data in transmission across a network.

It is also highly likely that in future, as the criminal and terrorist fraternity become more technologically aware, hacking will become a serious threat.

Safeguards

Security Modems. If you hold sensitive or confidential data on your system, and you are connected to a network - switch off the modem when you are not using it. If the modem has dial-in/out facilities then consider installing a "dial-back" modem. This will, if someone dials in to your system, disconnect the line and then dial back to the initiating system - it will only dial up authorised numbers.

Authentication. The two most widely used mechanisms to safeguard software or data in transmission are Encryption and Authentication. Encryption has been described earlier in this Chapter (and in Annex D). If the data or software is particularly sensitive, consider "authenticating" it prior to transmission. Authentication ensures that any changes made subsequently can be immediately detected.

Most authentication techniques work by the sending system performing a process on the data, producing a series of characters and/or numbers (known as a "key" or "seal") and appending that key to the data prior to transmission. The data itself is not encoded. The receiving system performs the same process calculating the key and comparing the new key with the key appended to the data. If the two keys differ, the data has been altered. Good authentication programs should be so sensitive that a change in one character of the program will cause a vast change in the key.

So, encryption will ensure that the wrongdoer cannot read the data, authentication will ensure that he cannot change it without detection. If the data itself is confidential, then it should be encrypted. If the data could be manipulated for gain - for example, financial data could be altered for fraudulent purposes - then it should be authenticated. If the data is confidential and financial, then it should be encrypted and authenticated.

Bear in mind, however, that encryption and authentication programs introduce overheads in time and system processing power, so should only be used on data or software *needing* protection.

CHAPTER 4

PROTECTION AGAINST FRAUD

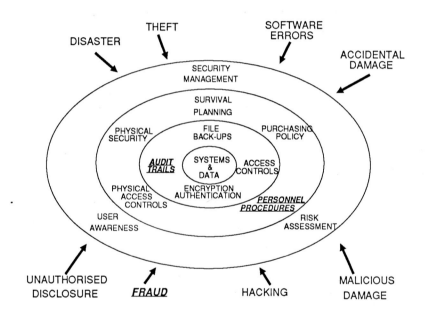

4.1   INTRODUCTION

Foreign Exchange markets in London transfer over 100 billion Pounds daily using EFT via satellite. The transactions take a very short time, and once completed there is no calling them back.

As more and more financial transactions are computerised, and more money is being transferred by electronic funds transfer (EFT), so computer fraud is increasing. Not only the number of frauds is increasing, the amounts stolen by computer fraud are higher than by conventional methods.

In America, over a six month period, there were 4,352 computer related thefts averaging $37,254 compared with 3,189 conventional frauds averaging only $6,270.

In many countries there is no statutory requirement to report computer crime. Most companies feel that the embarrassment and loss of public confidence following a publicised fraud would do the company more damage than the original crime. Consequently, frauds are not reported, and nobody really knows the true extent of the problem.

Types Of Fraud

The most common types of fraud are, in order of frequency of occurrence:

Manipulation of data: the incorrect input, or modification of data files that contain financial information, is a very common type of fraud. It can be protected against by controlling access to the data. However, on very small machines, like micro- computers, such controls are usually not built-in.

Unauthorised use of computer resources: the misuse of computer resources for private purposes, e.g. to run private programs, play games, or even provide private software bureaux.

Misuse of confidential data: knowledge of private company data stored on a computer system may be sufficient to provide the necessary information for fraud, or theft of data for resale (or ransom).

Software modifications: due to the level of specialisation and amount of effort needed, this type of fraud, is not very frequently encountered. It is however a very dangerous type of attack, since it may be very difficult to detect. Different types of software modifications have been identified; amongst the most well-known are: Trojan Horses, Salami Techniques, Logic Bombs (see Glossary of Terms for definition of these).

A contract programmer planted a series of logic bombs in the program code of a transport company system. Each time the program code was triggered it caused the system to fail. He was paid £350 to correct and restart the system each time.

The Fraudster

The basic ingredients for a fraud to be committed are motivation, knowledge of the system, opportunity to perpetrate the fraud, and something worth stealing. The most determining factor, and the most difficult to predict, however, remains the computer criminal himself. From the relatively small percentage of computer criminals that have been caught, some common characteristics have been identified.

Most computer crimes are committed by **internal personnel.** A minimum level of protection against outsiders is always present due to the location of the equipment in company buildings. This situation is somewhat different for networked systems, as will be discussed later.

Male perpetrators outnumber their female colleagues by a high ratio, and make higher profits.

The average **age** of the computer criminal is low. They hold a **position of trust** that gives them easy access to sensitive data, or the system in general. This does not imply that most criminals are computer people, many of them are users, working in financial sectors.

The highest value frauds are committed by managers; smaller crimes come from lower level personnel, but in larger numbers.

4.2 PERSONNEL PROCEDURES

Physical security and access controls provide an essential, basic level of protection against attempted fraud by outsiders. However, they do not provide protection against threats that come from within the authorised user group. Without honest, trustworthy personnel, all the effort and money spent in securing systems can be wasted.

We shall discuss in this section how you can improve security, by ensuring as far as is possible that only trustworthy people can access the computer system and that those who do not obey the rules are detected and appropriately disciplined.

Personnel security has many aspects, from choosing the right employees, through appropriate motivation and security training, to dealing with identified computer criminals. In large organisations with high data processing assets to be protected, it is advisable to have a security department to determine security policy and a strategy which includes personnel supervision and training.

Aspects of personnel security can be classified as follows:

* **Security policy for new employees**
* **Continuous personnel security program**
* **Personnel Control and Supervision**
* **Security policy for departing employees**

Security Policy for New Employees

How can a company looking for a new employee determine whether a person has the correct qualities?

Effective pre-employment screening can indicate security problems that might arise if a particular applicant were employed. The trustworthiness of a person can be estimated by means of a number of checks or tests; the more sensitive the position, the more effort should be spent in the screening process. It is impossible to have absolute certainty about the nature and intentions of an unknown person even using these techniques. Nevertheless, they should reduce the risk of hiring an untrustworthy employee.

Among well-known screening methods are:

Personality tests: Many companies use these tests, a number of which are available for establishing various characteristics of applicants. Make sure that the tests that are used meet the legal restrictions imposed by your country's labour laws.

Pre-employment interview: As part of the usual interview that is conducted, security related issues should be covered. Inform the applicant of the security policy within your company, of his future contractual obligations and of the consequences of disobeying the relevant company rules. Ask some direct questions about his employment history. If it appears that the applicant has behaved untrustworthily at a previous employer, or even if he appears to feel uncomfortable with this type of questioning, further background checking is a minimum requirement.

Background checking: These checks may vary from very elementary checks e.g. checking with previous employers, financial behaviour and criminal records, to an extensive investigation of the applicant's history by a specialised bureau. The cost of the investigation should be in accordance with the level of sensitivity of the related position.

The decision process: When making a decision upon hiring an applicant, all the information gathered during the screening process should be reviewed, checked and possible obscurities or inconsistencies identified. If necessary, to clear up some doubts, an additional interview may be conducted.

The above, while not pretending to guarantee personnel honesty, is very useful in eliminating those applicants from whom security problems could be expected.

Continuous Personnel Security Program

Establish a personnel security policy. This policy should encompass an identification of sensitive positions within the company and establish security education and motivation programs.

A Management Accountant pointed out flaws in his company's use of a new computer accounting system, and then proceeded to steal more than £1.5 million. He, and his accomplice (the accounts supervisor) both had unlimited security clearance.

Identification of Sensitive Positions: In general, the sensitivity of a position is based on the amount of damage that could be done by the fraudulent exploitation of functions of the position. Factors that may influence the sensitivity of a position are:

* The degree of accessibility to information.
* The degree of ability to effect sabotage.
* The degree to which activities can be performed without control from others.
* The level of security controls over the position.

Security Education and Motivation Programs: Security is not only the responsibility and task of management or security personnel. To achieve a high level of personnel security, it is essential that employees are aware of the risks of data processing and that they are motivated to assist in watching over the security of their computer systems.

A number of measures can be taken to stimulate such an attitude. First of all, supervisors should not only set the rules, but always set a good example themselves. Computer users should be informed regularly about the company's security policy: what actions are allowed or even encouraged, and what are prohibited. If employees are made aware of the need for security, they will be motivated to assist whenever they can. Motivation and job satisfaction play a key role in protection against fraud.

Personnel with security responsibilities should be given special education and training, so that they learn where and how to look for threats, and how to deal with them.

Personnel Control and Supervision

In an environment that currently tends towards more decentralisation (e.g. personal computers connected by a local area network), the task of supervision becomes even more difficult than before.

> *A bank clerk had sole charge of a branch mini-computer. She suppressed credits paid in by bank customers and redirected the money into accounts held by relatives and friends. To cover up the discrepancies she used the computer to re-type statements. The fraud was only discovered when a customer noticed that his bank balance was £25,000 less than it should have been.*

The following are key elements in effective personnel control and supervision:

Establish procedures to identify disgruntled employees: Problems should be dealt with in a smooth and positive fashion, or people will become deterred from revealing their feelings in the future. Security supervisors should be informed about possible disgruntled employees or situations which may render them disgruntled.

Separate job functions. The opportunity to commit a fraud undetected, often requires access to several separate company functions. Independent checking by different employees in different areas renders the opportunity and concealment of fraud difficult without collusion.

Avoid collusion by:

* Physical and administrative separation of different departments within a company.
* Rotation of duties: to decrease an employee's opportunity to breach the security of the system.
* Ensuring that at least two people are present when sensitive tasks are carried out.

Monitor for irregular activities and behaviour, unsupervised overtime working, illegal attempts to gain access into sensitive areas. Also watch for unusual
financial behaviour: people who are in financial trouble will more easily be
tempted to gain criminal profits; sudden extraordinary spending may indicate
such profits.

*A cashier embezzled more than £75,000 in a bid to regain the
affection of her adulterous husband by buying him presents
and taking him out for expensive meals.*

Performance appraisals should be given to all personnel, on a regular basis.
Management should ensure adequate remuneration, and also motivation and
career development to stimulate personnel co- operation and productivity.
Employees should be encouraged to discuss their feelings, including those of dissatisfaction.

Monitor personnel security tasks. Do this in such a way that honest
employees do not feel suspected or mistrusted, by, for example, explaining the
importance of the control and the necessity of the random character of the controls. No exceptions should be made.

Discipline security violators in an appropriate way. Details of disciplinary actions are company dependent and should be informed to new employees prior to
their joining the company.

Control system hardware and software modifications. New versions of
software should be checked for unauthorised amendments and tested properly
before instalment. During disaster recovery, when the use of backups is required, the integrity of software and data backups should be checked.

Security Policy for Departing Employees

The situation is quite different when the departing employee leaves of his own
free will, rather than being dismissed. However, to "play safe", follow the same
security procedures in both situations.

If an employee is dismissed for misconduct, incompetence or other cause, consider immediate dismissal. Although this may cost more, the elimination of

the risk of infliction of damage, out of revenge, may be of much higher value than the dubious performance that can be expected from an employee who is aware of his approaching involuntary departure.

Deny departing employees access to all computer facilities, including remote terminals, backup tapes, etc. Also, passwords and any other secret security codes and tokens, known or possessed by the departing employee, should be changed or collected, preferably before the subject is informed of his dismissal.

Inform colleagues about the employee departing, in order to assist in controlling the nature of his last activities. Last but not least, the departing employee should be reminded of his duties and responsibilities with respect to the company's security policy, to which he contractually agreed upon his acceptance as a new employee.

4.3 OPERATIONAL CONTROLS

Operational controls may be preventive, deterrent, detective, or a combination of these. They may be based on technical tools: software, hardware (e.g. access controls) or not (e.g. personnel procedures, security reviews). Software control tools may be incorporated in the computer's operating system (e.g. violation logging), or they may be available as separate software packages (e.g. auditing programs).

Most of the above controls are discussed elsewhere in this book - the remainder of this section will discuss security audit.

> *"Auditing is a systematic process of objectively obtaining and evaluating evidence regarding assertions about economic actions and events to ascertain the degree of correspondence between those assertions and established criteria, and communicating the results to interested users." (American Accounting Association Committee on Basic Auditing Concepts (1971).)*

This definition is not specifically tailored toward use in an electronic data processing (EDP) environment. Nevertheless, it can be explained for an EDP environment as follows:

Systematic Process: particularly in a complex environment such as the internal behaviour of a computer system, it is important to structure the auditing process in a logical manner to reduce the risk of neglecting important aspects of data or processing.

Objectively: Audits should be performed by independent people who have no prejudice about system weaknesses and who have no interest at all in falsifying the audit results.

Obtaining and Evaluating Evidence: An important number of audit-related processes are concerned with gathering information about events, which may serve as input for obtaining the desired audit results. Obtaining evidence regarding assertions requires both testing the system files for correctness and testing the compliance of the internal system controls.

Degree of correspondence: They are the outcome of the audit; they require some judgement on behalf of the auditor as to what should be considered as an internal control, non-compliance or a data inconsistency. This judgement requires a degree of competence due to the sophisticated nature of internal system controls and the difficulty of controlling data integrity

Computer Audit software

Key elements of EDP audit are the identification and review of internal EDP controls and the use of audit software to select, sample, analyse and compare information to assess these controls and to produce reports.

Before the introduction of data processing equipment, auditors reviewed data on paper. Computer equipment enabled the use of other means of data storage, to which fast on-line changes could be made. As a result auditors were forced to verify the integrity of this new environment with all its extended facilities, a complex and enormous task.

To alleviate the task of the auditor, specialised companies developed audit software programs, tailored to the specifications of most popular systems. The capabilities of these programs are so extended and varied that they cannot all be discussed here. Instead, a summary of the most important elements of commonly encountered audit programs will be presented.
The main types of programs are:

Logging and accounting programs: they are capable of logging almost any activity or event that occurs and to which they are triggered by the auditor. Examples are:

* Access violation logging
* Logging of (changes to) the security environment
* Activity logging of users
* Logging of unusual (eg: after hours) activities
* Logging the referencing of confidential information

Logging programs may provide indispensable input for audit trails and the analysis of transaction flows.

Control and examination programs: are used to detect and analyse inconsistencies between "proper computer behaviour" and the actual situation. Examples are:

* Checks on the file system: inadequately protected files or files with suspicious links, etc.
* Checking proper password usage.
* Checking presence and proper functioning of security controls or the equipment in general.

Data audit programs: sophisticated, multi-optional programs to extract, process and check specific file contents for data validity or inconsistencies, and make a report.

Source code comparison programs: compare the source code of different versions of software and report differences.

Audit trail and transaction flow analysis: trace the progress of transactions from their entry to the system until completion of the transaction. They report on irregularities that may have occurred during that process. This type of program usually requires that on-line track is kept of specific system activities.

4.4   IMPACT OF DIFFERENT TYPES OF SYSTEM

The protection methods discussed in this chapter are general in nature and applicable whatever the type of system in use. This does not imply that the system configuration and characteristics have no impact on the two main issues of this chapter: personnel procedures and operational controls.

Impact on Personnel Procedures

There is no direct relationship between the type of system and proper personnel procedures. The general principles explained previously remain valid.

However, applying these general principles to different working environments may impact on some of the previously mentioned personnel procedures.

When the introduction of new, less secure equipment, such as micro-computers or Local Area Networks introduces changes to the overall amount and distribution of risk, then the personnel procedures should be checked and changed if necessary to bring, for example, job sensitivities and controls, into line with the new situation.

Impact on Operational Controls

In contrast with personnel procedures, operational controls are determined to a much greater extent by the available equipment. EDP audit features are mainly applicable to medium and large size systems, such as mini-computers and mainframes.

Manufacturers rarely provide security controls on small systems like micro-computers and word processors. The reason for this is very straightforward: the major concern of a manufacturer is to survive in the very competitive market of microsystems. The provision of more security than a simple physical lock, will inevitably raise prices and reduce processing capability.

If you need a higher level of security for your micro-computer, there are a whole range of add-on security products, as software encryption packages, or extension boards for access control and file encryption. However, few products have been developed for the audit and control of small systems.

From a security point of view, the use of small systems can be summarised as follows:

* Small systems are inherently insecure, due to their restricted processing capabilities and easily accessible resources.
* As a consequence, it may be inadvisable to use this equipment for the processing and storage of sensitive financial information.
* Micro-computer security can be improved with generally available extension boards and other tools. However, in general , these are not user- friendly and slow down processing.
* Micro-computer security review and audit is usually restricted to the use of non-technical controls, e.g. of physical and procedural nature.

The use of security review questionnaires and checklists are recommended to review your awareness of risks and appropriate safeguards. A review checklist of micro-computer security should encompass at least the following elementary topics to protect against fraud:

* Control and security of (sensitive) data: secure storage of diskettes (originals and backups), protection of downloaded mainframe data, privacy and integrity protection by file encryption.
* Conformance with software vendors' regulations on proprietary software, to reduce legal risks.
* Aspects of physical security: protection against unauthorised access, sabotage, theft.
* User awareness of possible risks induced by the inherent lack of security of small computers.

CHAPTER 5

SURVIVAL PLANNING

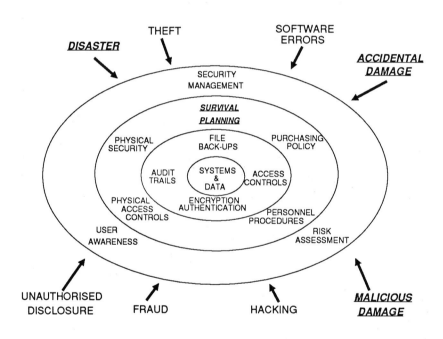

5.1   INTRODUCTION

Previous chapters of this book have described safeguards to prevent or deter various disasters, minor or major. But no safeguard is always 100% effective. Accidents will happen, however well protected your system might be.

What would happen if your computer system disappeared right now? If your reply is "nothing", or "I'd put my back-up files on my spare machine and carry on" then you can probably ignore this chapter. (Although, do not forget to check out the spare machine regularly to ensure that it is still compatible with your software and data).

What can be done to minimise the effect of a disaster if it does happen? The answer is simple - draw up a plan for recovery from disaster - a Survival Plan - and follow it in the event of disaster.

Depending on the size and complexity of your system, the plan may vary from straightforward simple instructions on a single sheet of paper through to a full Survival Plan Manual detailing individual actions and responsibilities subsequent to a disaster.

For example, if your system is a stand-alone micro-computer or word processor your "survival plan" could be brief notes on what to do if the hardware (or software) fails, i.e.:

* Address and phone number of supplier and procedures for repair.
* Address and phone number of software supplier/distributor.
* Location of a spare, compatible machine, or a distributor from whom one can be obtained at short notice.

Note: Please check, regularly, that you can still obtain spare parts or a compatible system - computing equipment is evolving rapidly, and you may well find, if your system has been in use for a few years, that replacement is not possible.

At the other end of the spectrum, a network of micro-computers and mini- computers could need a full, detailed, documented Survival Plan, particularly if the company relies on the system to function.

This chapter will describe full Survival Planning (and testing) - some of the topics may not be applicable for your system, but do consider all the factors mentioned when drawing up your plan. In particular, use the suggested Survival Plan contents in Annex F as a checklist for your plan.

Effect Of Disaster

The basic reasons for investing in a Survival Plan are that the risk of experiencing a disaster is increasing (particularly in the areas of man-made and environmental disasters) and that the time available to respond and recover is being dramatically reduced.

The emergence of inexpensive computing power, packaged software and the ability to house sophisticated equipment in a normal office environment, means that small companies are able to take advantage of computers to control their business in a way previously only possible for large concerns. The problem is that many such small companies have little experience of data processing, its dangers, or compensating security controls and procedures. They may also have limited resources available to enable them to overcome and recover from a disaster should one occur.

A recent report showed that where organisations have suffered a disaster to their computing system and did not have a survival plan, less than seven per cent were still in business after five years.

The effect of a disaster on someone controlling his major business functions and keeping his business records on a small computer system in an office environment could be just as devastating.

Insurance

One important aspect of planning for recovery from any disaster is to insure against loss of your system. The type, scope and value of the policy that you take out will depend very much on the size, complexity and function of your computer system. But whatever its size, when deciding on the amount of cover required do remember again to estimate the total value of the system - not just the hardware. Also, review your insurance requirements regularly - the value of your hardware may or may not be increasing, but the value of the whole system to your company is almost certainly increasing with time.
(Note: keep written details of the type of equipment, including serial numbers, in case of theft.)

5.2   APPROACHES TO SURVIVAL PLAN DEVELOPMENT

There are, basically, three approaches to developing a survival plan. You could adopt a do-it-yourself approach, purchase a methodology book or use specialised consultants.

Do-it-Yourself. Such an approach requires considerable resources to decide how to develop the plan, what it needs to cover, the way in which it should be structured and the many tasks which need to be done during survival (which could be overlooked by someone inexperienced in such planning). There are also the problems of adequately training the staff in the use of the plan, and of practically testing it.

For smaller organisations, with simple plan requirements, a do-it-yourself approach should be most effective. However, do investigate the resourcing required and the economics, carefully.

Methodology Book. There are books which describe a methodology for developing a survival plan. These books often contain the forms to be used to collect the necessary data. Some companies will write the plan from the data collected while some will lease or sell a computer program into which the data is fed in order to produce a plan automatically.

The major advantage to using such an approach is that the price to be paid to the outside company is relatively small. Take care, however, when considering this approach, to make an estimate of the total costs (including those which will be incurred internally).

Specialised Consultants. There are a growing number of consultants with expertise in survival planning. The disadvantage of using specialised consultants is the higher external cost involved. The advantages are:

* **many of the consultants will manage the development to ensure both its timely completion and minimum impact on your normal workload.**
* **there is a marriage between the consultants experience of survival planning and your knowledge of your own business, producing a plan which is unique and tailored to your requirements.**

5.3   THE SURVIVAL PLAN

Disaster is an unanticipated interruption of business activities for any reason. Survival, recovery from the disaster, requires a plan of action designed to minimise the disruption of key business operations. In preparing the plan it is important to realise that disaster and the subsequent recovery may not be a brief event. You may have to operate in a recovery mode for anything from weeks to months depending on the duration of the interruption and the extent of the damage. The plan of action will include detailed procedures to be followed during the survival activity, together with a list of resources required and where these are kept ready for use.

Part of the process of developing the plan is to force the decisions which must be taken in order to survive to be made before the disaster occurs. There are two main reasons why the procedures must be very detailed and for forcing the early decision making. The first is that it is possible that key employees may be absent during the disaster and that their place may have to be taken by alternative personnel who, although trained, may not be as adept as the primary personnel. The second reason is that if normal business is disrupted, and procedures change suddenly, it is easier and more efficient for people to adhere to new procedures if they are detailed and documented.

Basic Requirements for a Plan

There are certain basic requirements, common to all Survival Plans, which must be met if the plan is to provide adequate, ongoing protection. These are:

There must be **top management commitment** to the process. This is essential for three reasons: first, because they will have final approval for budget and resource requirements; second, because they will decide when to implement the survival plan and at what level, and third, because top management are most effective in enlisting the support of all necessary departments throughout the company.

It must plan for the **worst-case situation.** One misconception is that it is necessary to know the degree of risk from various possible types of disaster. Although this is necessary to some extent during the prevention activity it is not necessary during survival planning. It does not matter what has caused the "disaster", the necessity is to survive it.

It must be **modular** because although the plan is designed to cope with a total disaster, in many cases the disasters which occur will be minor or intermediate in nature. It should only be necessary to activate those modules needed to cope with what has occurred.

The survival plan should be **structured** so that each individual need only know, be trained in, and be able to use, his or her section of the plan.

Even in the simplest plan for a small company there are several areas of activity or functions which should be considered and addressed where necessary:

* **Management/Administration**
* **Transportation**
* **New Equipment**
* **Technical Support**
* **Communications**
* **Security**
* **Alternate Computer Systems**
* **Data Preparation**
* **Personnel**

Developing the Plan

The first step in developing the plan itself is to decide which functions are so critical that if they are not re-started within one or two days then the business simply cannot survive. Then other activities must be assessed by arriving at the financial or operational impact to the organisation of their loss.

The second step is to define the different tasks that have to be performed if survival is to be achieved, and to assign them to people, by job function. Many of these are unique to the survival situation and unknown in the day-to-day work situation. Many are also unique to the company concerned and will depend on its specific survival requirements.

The third step is to develop the detailed procedures and establish the resources necessary to do these jobs and the fourth is to document steps one, two and three into a plan.

Steps two, three and four - task definition, procedure and resource development and plan documentation - are not necessarily performed in sequence with each step completed before the next starts. They should be, in fact, an ongoing loop of activities leading to continuous expansion and refinement.

There are two main reasons for adopting this iterative method of developing the plan.

The first is that it assists in establishing planning as a part of the everyday working methodology. People are more likely to realise when something changes that the survival plan is affected and must also be brought up-to-date. The second is that it is the basic method of employee training. Involvement in the gradual expansion in the detail of the plan leads to the instinctive understanding of it which enables its successful implementation.

Finally, during plan development, the people not included in the current plan should be educated as to their exposure, their needs in protecting themselves and future plans for expanding the plan to include their function.

Testing and Maintenance

The development of a Survival Plan is not a one-off task which can be considered as complete once the first draft is finished. There are three more critical components of successful planning and these are, training, testing and maintenance.

Training: the staff who will have to carry out and manage the survival process must be thoroughly trained so that they can carry out their part in the plan. In practice this means that it is desirable that the people who will have to use the plan should be involved in its development.

Testing is mandatory to ensure success and is the acid check on whether the plan is workable; of details which may have been overlooked; of timing expectations; of alternate site compatibility and whether back up routines are adequate.

There are many different aspects that can and should be tested. Some examples of these are:

* The procedures to notify everybody that needs to know and to activate the plan.
* The ability to conduct damage assessment. In other words to estimate the extent to which the proper functioning of the organisation will be affected and for how long.
* How well applications or business functions can run on the alternate system.

There should be a set of objectives to be met for each test and detailed documentation of what was done, by whom, the results and what the implications are for future testing activity.

Maintenance of the Survival Plan is also vital. The plan must be continuously updated whenever there is a change in such elements as the hardware, a change in personnel or supplier, the criticality of an application, the introduction of a new system or communications.

Suggested Contents for a full Survival Plan can be found in Annex F. Use this as a checklist - not all of it will apply to your circumstances.

5 . 4   ALTERNATIVE SYSTEM SELECTION

Since the basic guideline in developing the Survival Plan is "Plan for the worst" the plan should always include the procedures for using an alternative system, possible in another location. Options include reciprocal agreement, a replacement system, a standby system, service bureau.

Reciprocal Agreement. This is an agreement between the users of two or more compatible systems that if one experiences a major interruption in processing then the other(s) will provide back up facilities. For example, a back-up for a stand-alone micro-computer could be an identical machine (with the same software installed) in another office.

The primary apparent advantage is economy. There are, however, drawbacks. As each system progresses it becomes increasingly difficult to ensure that hardware and software remain compatible, or both systems could experience the same disaster. Additionally, and not infrequently, it will seldom be convenient for the user of the back-up system to hand-over his system at short notice. You may be forced to work distinctly unsociable hours until you have your own system again.

Replacement System. When disaster occurs the hardware equipment supplier is called upon for replacement equipment. (You would be advised to have an agreement with the vendor to supply replacement equipment readily, at short notice.) This can work very well for small stand-alone systems, or local area networks where all the equipment is supplied by one vendor.

Standby System. This option can be provided by specialist suppliers who offer their clients a facility on continuous standby. Alternatively, maintain your own "standby system" by keeping a compatible (hardware and software) system separate from your system, and using your stored back-up data to recover. The advantages of this option include ready availability and security.

Service Bureau. Using a commercial service bureau can have the advantages of immediate availability and the economy of only having to pay for the time used. Long term processing at a service bureau is, however, very expensive. Security considerations, testing and ensuring the ready availability of sufficient capacity can also be problems.

If you can tolerate being without your system for perhaps days then a replacement system may be perfectly acceptable. As the time required to respond and recover becomes more critical, however, then reciprocal agreement or a "standby system" would be advisable.

CHAPTER 6

RISK ASSESSMENT

6.1   INTRODUCTION

The previous chapters in this book have offered varied advice on how to protect your system and its software and data from various threats. But how can you assess whether your system is at risk from the threats discussed?

The remainder of this chapter describes a quick and easy method of assessing your risks. This method is designed to assess the risks facing a single system, or, perhaps, a small number of systems in a section or department within an organisation. It is not recommended for analysing threats or assessing risk for larger computer systems or for a whole organisation.

6.2 RISK ASSESSMENT

Asset Evaluation. First list the component parts of your system (hardware and software) and assign values to them. Then use the questions in 3.2 to assess how valuable the data is - you may not be able to calculate a precise monetary value, but a measure of the protection the data needs (if any) should be apparent.

Threat Analysis. Using photocopies of the threat sheets at the end of this chapter, tick in the appropriate column for each threat on the list. While doing this, try to think of any other threats to which your system could be vulnerable, and include them. This should give you a measure of how likely a threat's occurrence is - ie the risk of it's happening.

Safeguard Selection. In the right hand column by each threat is a list of safeguards. (Each of the safeguards mentioned is described in this book).

If the level of risk is high or medium (columns 1 or 2 ticked) consider implementing one or more of the safeguard(s) listed against the threat, if they are cost-effective. Their cost- effectiveness will depend on the (financial) value you placed on the asset, and the cost of implementing the safeguard.

If the level of risk is low (column 3 or 4 ticked) consider implementing safeguards only if the asset is valuable or needs protecting for some other reason (for example, it is difficult to replace or re-create, or it is data which could cause embarrassment to the company if disclosed). Again check that it is cost-effective.

If you have ticked column 5 you can probably ignore the threat - unless the asset is of very high value or irreplaceable.

Existing Safeguards. When selecting safeguards, look at existing conditions - check that implementing a new safeguard would not nullify or reduce the effectiveness of existing safeguards.

While assessing your risks, and considering safeguards, remember - maintain a sense of proportion (good security is 70% common sense) and implement the controls and procedures that your system needs.

THREAT

Theft

Threat	HAPPENING NOW (1)	POSSIBLE-HAS HAPPENED (2)	POSSIBLE-NOT HAPPENED (3)	UNLIKELY (4)	NEVER (5)	SAFEGUARDS	PAGE REF.
Theft of equipment or Components						Lock and key	9
By outsiders						Alarms Security awareness	9 9
By insiders						Inventory Restrict access	9 9
Theft of Data/Software						Lock and key Access controls	9 23-28
By outsiders						Encryption Authentication	28 39
By insiders						File back-ups Switch off modems	22 39

THREAT **Deliberate damage**	HAPPENING NOW 1	POSSIBLE :- HAS HAPPENED 2	POSSIBLE :- NOT HAPPENED 3	UNLIKELY 4	NEVER 5	SAFEGUARDS	PAGE REF:
Deliberate damage to equipment/components						Restrict access Security awareness Survival planning	12 9 54-63
By outsiders						Lock and key Alarms T.V. surveillance	9 9 12
By insiders						Lock and key Personnel procedures	12 43
To data/software						Access controls Lock and key	23-28 22
By outsiders						Security awareness File back-ups	9 22
By insiders						Authentication	39

THREAT **Accidental damage**	HAPPENING NOW 1	POSSIBLE :- HAS HAPPENED 2	POSSIBLE :- NOT HAPPENED 3	UNLIKELY 4	NEVER 5	SAFEGUARDS	PAGE REF:
Accidental damage to equipment/components						Equipment movement Survival planning	10 54-63
						Dust covers	10
By outsiders						Restrict access	22
By insiders						Restrict access	22
To data/software						Access controls Lock and key Restrict facilities	23-28 12 22
By outsiders						File back-ups	17,22
By insiders						Authentication	39

THREAT	HAPPENING NOW	POSSIBLE:- HAS HAPPENED	POSSIBLE:- NOT HAPPENED	UNLIKELY	NEVER	SAFEGUARDS	PAGE REF:
	1	2	3	4	5		
Unauthorised disclosure							
Unauthorised disclosure							
Of Confidential data						Encryption	28
Personal data						Access controls	23-28
Financial data							
Other data							
By Staff						Access controls	23-28
Accidental viewing						Screen position Lock and key	13 13
Waste disposal						Shredding/burning	13
Hacking						Switch off modems Encryption	13 28
Other							

THREAT — Fraud	HAPPENING NOW 1	POSSIBLE:- HAS HAPPENED 2	POSSIBLE:- NOT HAPPENED 3	UNLIKELY 4	NEVER 5	SAFEGUARDS	PAGE REF:
Fraud							
By Insiders						Personnel procedures	43
Changing software						Access controls / Authentication	23-28 / 39
Changing data						Audit programs / Encryption	51 / 28
Changing documents						Restrict access	43
By Outsiders							
Changing software						Access controls / Authentication	23-28 / 39
Changing data						Audit programs / Encryption	51 / 28
Changing documents						Restrict access	43
Other							

THREAT — Environmental	HAPPENING NOW — 1	POSSIBLE:- HAS HAPPENED — 2	POSSIBLE:- NOT HAPPENED — 3	UNLIKELY — 4	NEVER — 5	SAFEGUARDS	PAGE REF:
Fire, major						Fire extinguisher Fire proof safes Automatic controls	16 12, 16 16
Fire, minor						Survival planning Housekeeping rules	54-63 16
Flood, plumbing						Siting of equipment Survival planning	17 54-63
Flood, weather						Siting of equipment Survival planning	17 54-63
Power fluctuation						Stabiliser	17
Power cut						Battery back-up Alternate power supply	17 17
Static electricity						Anti-static spray Anti-static mats	17 17
Earthquake						Backup files Survival planning	17,22 54-63
Storm damage						Unplug equipment Survival planning	16 54-63
Other							

CHAPTER 7

SECURITY MANAGEMENT—
AN ORGANISATIONAL VIEW

7.1   INTRODUCTION

The previous chapters of this book have, generally, addressed the end-user of a small computer system - the accountant, secretary, clerk, doctor, lawyer etc. who is actually controlling and using one or more systems. Some of the controls and procedures described may need, by their nature, to be implemented company-wide (for example, personnel procedures in Chapter 4), some can be installed on individual systems.

If the management of computer security throughout a company is left to individuals or departments, the end result is usually a piece-meal security implementation - over-protection in some areas, under-protection in others. In order to install and manage security cost-effectively, the company as a whole should install and maintain a coherent security programme. Basic "good housekeeping" rules to enhance security, such as those described in Chapter 2 should be uniform throughout the organisation.

This final chapter provides guidelines for managing security within the organisation. No two companies are alike, so these guidelines are written at a level such that they can be adapted to suit your organisation. Seven areas are discussed:

* **The place of computer security in the business.**
* **Risk management.**
* **Computer security policy.**
* **Implementing the policy.**
* **The integration of computer security with system development.**
* **The acquisition and management of systems.**
* **The management of change.**

7.2 THE PLACE OF COMPUTER SECURITY IN THE BUSINESS

Computer security is often seen as, and introduced as, a separate measure. Frequently the approach to computer security bears little relationship to the approach to security that may exist elsewhere in the organisation.

Security should be applied as a consistent company policy which includes all business functions, as well as functions carried out on computer systems. Computer security should be an integral part of any organisation's approach to security.

Computer systems, small and large, generally provide support to a business function - which will have its own aims and strategy. Responsibility for the business functions lies with senior executives (usually), and the task of assuring the security and credibility of the business function is usually included in this responsibility. As business functions become increasingly dependent on small computer systems, the responsibility for their security should be recognised.

Frequently security is managed from too far down in the organisation. The authority needed to induce a positive security commitment is therefore lacking. Security officers frequently do not have the authority to develop an effective policy, let alone implement and control it.

Security should be managed from a senior position in the organisation, so that the security approach adopted can be evenly applied across the organisation. Computer security can then be managed in this organisational context.

Before addressing computer security specifically, examine your company's approach to security as a whole.

If you are not satisfied with your company's general approach, seek first to introduce a security culture to provide the necessary context for computer security. This means devising and mounting a specific program for ensuring that the people concerned are aware of, and observe, these new responsibilities.

Personnel, faced with new security related tasks which at first sight seem more trouble than they are worth, will respond more positively if the new responsibilities are fully explained in terms of the organisation's business and security objectives. In effect, the end-user must be sold the benefits of security.

7.3   RISK MANAGEMENT

Striking the right balance between expenditure and level of protection is one of the most important and difficult elements in security management.

How should you decide what level of computer security to impose? Security can be expensive.

The decision can be governed by the disciplines of Risk Analysis. The process of risk analysis should provide the objective equation between expenditure on, and return from, security.

Risk Analysis techniques may be used to examine the exposure to risk of a computer system including its fixed and tangible assets, facilities and personnel. The risk is the likelihood that an adverse event will occur, and the impact is the consequences of that adverse event occurring. Adverse events, or threats, include hardware failures, human errors, natural disasters, unauthorised access to confidential or personal information and many others.

Where both the likelihood and the impact are "low" in relation to other potential threats, there may only be a need to formally recognise this at a lower priority. In the case where either the likelihood or the impact is "high", there may be cause for concern and an evaluation of countermeasures should be undertaken.

Where both likelihood and impact are "high", high priority should be given to the reduction of either, or both, and countermeasures should be evaluated and selected for implementation at the earliest opportunity. The evaluation of countermeasures is a process whereby the investment in safeguards or protective measures is offset against the reduction in risk exposure.

7.4 SECURITY POLICY

There is a danger that an organisation may attempt a piecemeal implementation of security measures, not as elements in a coherent and planned policy. Many organisations do not recognise the need to define common security objectives and measure their success in obtaining these objectives.

The diagram (Figure 7.1) shows a Security Management Cycle for Small Systems. Although the terminology differs, elements of this cycle are evident in most organisations. However, the last stage - evaluating progress - is frequently omitted. For this reason many organisations regard the security of small systems as an almost unobtainable moving target.

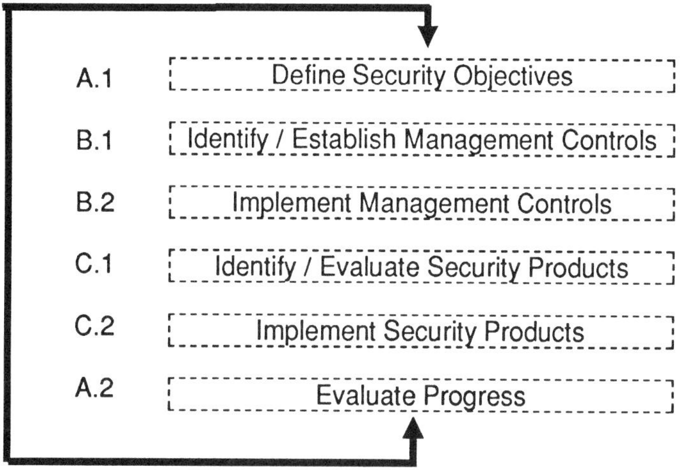

A.1   Define Security Objectives

B.1   Identify / Establish Management Controls

B.2   Implement Management Controls

C.1   Identify / Evaluate Security Products

C.2   Implement Security Products

A.2   Evaluate Progress

FIGURE 7.1: SMALL SYSTEMS SECURITY MANAGEMENT CYCLE

Note the pairing of A.1 and A.2 - defining the target with a corresponding measure of achievement. A similar pairing is implied with B.1 and B.2 and C.1 and C.2. Note also that the process is iterative and will be carried out many times over.

A Security Policy is a formal statement of intent issued by senior management. It comprises a definition of the objectives, which they have determined are necessary for the organisation for the successful pursuit of its business. It is a pre-requisite for successful security policy definition that equally substantive business and technical policies exist.

The policy is attained by discussions between the business, technical and security executives supported by a committee drawn from line management to represent the interests and spectrum of activities of the organisation.

Measuring the effectiveness of a security policy is a continuing process. In order to create the least resistance to the measurement process it needs to be a natural outcome of existing practices and reports.   At the highest level the existence of a security committee should help to focus the receipt and distribution of general security information. For more specific matters, where a need-to-know concept may apply, it is essential to have a Security Manager. He should have resources in the form of one or more divisional staff per division responsible to him for security matters which require the immediacy of response not normally associated with a committee.

In order to assess the effectiveness it will be necessary to measure the extent of attainment of the goals of the policy. For this reason it is essential that the goals are set in measurable terms.

The first measurable criteria is the number of incidents which constitute a breach of the rules which sustain the policy. For instance, if part of the policy relates to physical security and requires doors to be locked at night, and there is a higher than acceptable incidence of non-compliance from one division this would indicate the need for action. A review of the circumstances might indicate the need for training, stiff penalties, or automatic locks. Similar measures can be derived for all feasible requirements.

The second measurable criteria is cost. When the process of getting the number of incidents (of all types) down to a reasonable level has been successful it is appropriate to concentrate on reducing the ongoing cost of maintaining that level. Prior to that the capital (and running) cost of an objective may have to be borne.

The third measurable criteria is industry comparison. This is evidently a more indirect measure since industry reporting may be neither timely nor wholly truthful. A good indicator could be insurance fees but this indicator requires specialist knowledge since other factors are involved.

Since security is an abstract quality, it is often related to a sense of well-being or belief in one's immunity against life's minor (or major) disasters. There is little or no place for such complacency in a formal security policy since we cannot measure the underlying judgement.

It can be reasoned that security is an alternative form of gambling, the higher the stakes the more likely the opponents will chicken out, but there is always someone who will figure an angle on how to improve his odds of beating your security procedures. It is important to measure your own preparedness for the unusual and wherever possible to learn from the mistakes of your competitors. This is an important but indirect indicator of the extent to which your security intelligence keeps you ahead of the competition. Judging how far to go on expending resources for intelligence and subsequent responses to perceived potential threats is a fine art and needs to be tempered by the business and technical risks that are acceptable to Senior Management.

7.5 IMPLEMENTING THE POLICY

Having developed a coherent security policy relevant to your business, you then have to develop and implement a strategy to fulfil the objectives of the policy.

Ensure that a status review is carried out to establish a base from which progress can be measured. This review must be sufficiently detailed that you can be satisfied that all aspects have been considered.

The Security Status review should include:-

Organisation	- Structure - Culture - Security Management - Management - Use of data processing (now and future plans) - Business functions - Information held (data classes)
Risk review	- Risks present - Vulnerabilities

From the results of the review, and the stated policy objectives, a Security Strategy can be drawn up. This strategy should include:

* **Identification of Security roles and responsibilities**
* **Security Management**
* **Information Security (Data Classification and protection)**
* **Contingency planning**
* **System Development/purchase**
* **Personnel Procedures**
* **Physical Security (building and systems)**
* **Risk Management**
* **Security Standards**

The final part of the Strategy document should be a detailed plan showing costs and timescales for implementing the Strategy.

Ensure that people with the right experience in implementing security plans - not necessarily those who drew up the plan - are in charge of and conduct its implementation.

Ensure that security procedures are properly operated, logged and duly audited internally.

Ensure that there is regular feedback from users and that the strategy remains sufficiently dynamic to be able to respond to adverse criticisms or new requirements: otherwise the strategy will be circumvented and lose its value. That is ensure that adequate experienced resources are kept available to handle such feedback - the strategy cannot respond on its own.

7.6 INTEGRATION OF SECURITY AND SYSTEM DEVELOPMENT

Computer security must be included from the beginning. Trying to retrofit security, even where this is possible, can often be done only at great cost and operating disruption. Retrofitted security is seldom as effective as when integrally developed with the system.

How do you integrate the development of security features to control a system, with that of the system itself?

The danger is not so much the obvious one, that this integration will not take place, but that it will be inadequately conducted. Integrating security may cut right across many procedures the user employs in system development: use of external packages - problems of choice, integration and support; or allowing each system to develop its own security features - which may integrate well with the rest of the system's software, but which will result in fragmented security procedures across the organisation.

The first recommendation must be to decide which security features should be injected into the systems in the organisation: features such as access controls and other internal control checks, as opposed to external security features such as physical protection, planning for disaster recovery.

These features should also include standard checkpoint/recovery procedures for use in all programmes, to enable the system (i) to recover from failure or malfunctions of hardware or software, (ii) to enable its files and processes to be reconstituted if a disaster strikes. Such checkpointing features are further addressed in 7.7 overleaf.

Decide on how those features should be implemented: by buying a commercial package off-the-shelf or by developing specific software. What hardware is required, eg to govern access control, prevent illegal copying etc and what is on the market? Then draw up a plan to implement coherent security measures on all the systems in the company.

You should then be in a position to coordinate the development planning of both your security features and your system. Figure 7.2 illustrates the process overall; note especially the importance of regular reviews, training and, above all, testing.

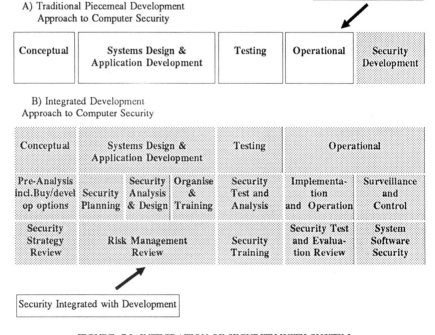

FIGURE 7.2 INTEGRATION OF SECURITY WITH SYSTEM

7.7 ACQUIRING A SYSTEM

This book primarily addresses computer security safeguards designed to protect the computer system from malevolent or accidental attack, or from natural disasters.

This chapter would not be complete, however, unless it also addressed a different set of threats and vulnerabilities: normal failures (ie breakdowns and malfunctions) of the system. These reflect the characteristics of the hardware and software themselves.

How should you manage the acquisition and operation of a system that will give you, cost effectively, the spread and quality of service that you require?

Ideally you should:

* **Develop the system according to documented and well tried rules that enable you to manage your commitment of funds to the project, and at the same time to get value for money out of its development;**

* **Provide specifications for the system that align with business objectives, or enable you to take practical advantage of new technology.**

* **Realise the increasing importance of systems to the continuance/profitability of your business. Do not take for granted such crucial factors as: the level of performance needed, the amount of failure that can be tolerated in the system's operation, the recovery mechanisms from a failure that should be incorporated, or the level of confidentiality to be applied.**

*   Realise the impact of trends in the marketing of system products, particularly at the level of microsystems where hardware and software tend to be bought off the shelf. This mostly impacts the smaller business users, those likely to have the least access to professional advice and support.

*   Realise the importance of imposing rigorous testing and commissioning on all products: for system and site environment hardware, for all categories of software - whether developed in-house or bought-in as one or more packages, and for all user/operating procedures.

The management guidelines we suggest align with the above:

*   Life-Cycle: Figure 7.2 illustrates the integration of security into the system development life-cycle. This cycle should be equally applied to all system development, whether simple or complex, whether the system is to be made up primarily of bought-in products or developed in-house.

*   Specifications: strike the most sensible balance between excessive caution and ambition. This is a qualitative judgement, but should be governed by on the one hand, the current and projected requirements of the business, and on the other, the ability of management to retain control.

*   Performance and Recovery: compile a realistic picture of the workload to be handled - transactions-in, reports, storage, volumes of queries; leave 100% margin for expansion and Parkinsons Law.

*   *Do not ignore* the need to inject checkpoint facilities to enable you to restart your system without loss of data after a failure.

* Vendors: Buying off-the-shelf or through dealers may be cheaper initially than developing your own system (or part of it) or having it developed by a reputable system vendor: but can incur significant later cost for you.

* Establish early a firm policy on which vendor products to use, and insist that any deviations are justified.

* Testing and Commissioning: Test all products in your own environment before you accept them. Many products, particularly software, may not be sufficiently tested before reaching the market.

Finally, remember the importance of keeping your staff well motivated: personnel packages and policies; information; precise allocation of responsibilities; sensible application of clearly understood sanctions.

7.8 CONTROLLING CHANGE

No system remains static. There will always be change: minor changes to existing requirements, new requirements altogether, desire to use proven more cost effective technology.

How do you recognise the problem, and institute the best combination of management and operational procedures to contain it?

It can be dangerous to refuse to recognise not just the need to manage change, but the scale of penalties for not doing so. These will directly affect the secure running of the system and therefore, probably, of the business: uncontrolled amendments to operating programs; lack of control over passwords and user privileges in access control; outdated distribution lists for reports; documentation not reflecting software or operating procedures, ... the list is endless.

Modern techniques for change-management centre on Configuration Control. It is essentially simple: the painstaking recording of the status of all assets to be controlled: hardware, software, procedures, access lists, etc and the mandatory recording of all changes to this status.

* Clearly identify all categories of assets to be controlled. Figure 7.3 identifies typical categories, and applies equally to single system or multiple system installations.

* Tabulate the items to be initially registered under each category; identification, brief text, version, date- of-last-change, who is responsible.

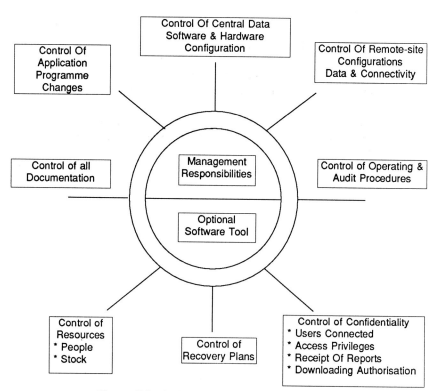

Figure 7.3: the Importance Of Managing Change
Permeates The Management Of Security

*   Consider the frequency with which each asset category, or
     key items within a category, will change.

*   Develop a system to record this information, register all re-
     quested changes, inform all relevant people of the likely ef-
     fect of a change if implemented, ensure that any effected
     change is consistently recorded in all the categories it may af-
     fect. This applies particularly to application software chan-
     ges - not only changes to the software but to its documenta-
     tion, and possibly also to operating procedures, other
     software etc: the ramifications may be considerable but
     should be carefully tracked down and recorded.

*   Ensure that precise operating procedures are developed for
     the change management functions; and that one (or more)
     staff are charged with being responsible for them, for their ef-
     fective operation, and for keeping them up-to-date.

*   Finally mandate that all requests for changes be registered
     for analysis and approval, and then - if approved - imple-
     mented according to this function's procedures.

ANNEX A

ACKNOWLEDGEMENTS

The consortium of companies participating in the MAP 1018 project "Security for Small and Medium Sized Systems" would like to thank the following companies for their valuable assistance and information input to the project:

Philips International BV
Midland Bank plc
The Littlewoods Organisation plc
Tandem Computers Ltd
Ing C Olivetti & Co SpA
IBM (UK) Ltd
British Airways
ICL
Data General Ltd
Siemens AG
Department of Trade and Industry (UK)
Central Computer and Telecommunications Agency (UK)
Digital Equipment Co Limited
Honeywell Information Systems Ltd
Ministerie Van Justitie (Netherlands)
Director of the Data Inspectorate (Norway)
Der Hessische Daten Schutzbeanftragte (West Germany)
Touche Ross & Co
Logica (UK) Ltd
Sypro
Inmos Ltd
Nokia IJ
John Bell Technical Services Ltd
Price Waterhouse
Respite Services Ltd
Cotag International Ltd
Racal-Guardata Ltd
Concord-Eracom Computer GmbH

Peat Marwick Mitchell and Co
Micro-computer Advisory Services
NCR Limited
Systems Designers plc
Mannesmann Kienzle GmbH
Cifer plc
TSB Scotland plc
Cable and Wireless plc
Kent County Council
RMC Group plc
Istel Group Ltd
Petroquimica E Gas de Portugal EP
Institute of Internal Auditors (UK)
Correios E Telecommunicacoes de Portugal
Austin Rover Group Ltd
Analytical Instruments Ltd
Rank Xerox Ltd
3M Italia SpA
Lazard Brothers & Co Limited
John Sisk & Son Ltd
Warren Spring Laboratory
Phillips Petroleum Co Ltd
Industrial Development Authority (Ireland)
EXOR SA
The Boots Company plc
Institute of Management Services
Society for Computers and Law
Institute of Data Processing Management
ECOMA
Commercial Union Risk Management Ltd

ANNEX B

GLOSSARY OF TERMS

ACCESS CONTROL: The process of limiting access to the resources of data processing systems only to authorised users, programs, processes, or other data processing systems (in computer networks).

AUDIT TRAIL: A chronological record of system activities which is sufficient to enable the reconstruction, review and examination of the sequence of environments and activities surrounding or leading to each event in the path of a transaction from its inception to output of final results.

ACCESS RIGHTS: The functions and data to which a user has access and the abilities (read, update, etc.) he has to act on those functions or data.

AUTHENTICATION A: The act of verifying the purported identity of an originator or individual.

B: A measure designed to provide protection against fraudulent transmissions by establishing the validity of a transmission, message, or originator.

BACK-UP
PROCEDURES: The provisions made for the recovery of data files and program libraries, and for restart or replacement of DP equipment after the occurrence of a system failure or of a disaster.

CONTINGENCY:

Arrangements, consisting of plans, instructions and physical facilities to resort to an alternative mode of operation in the event of a denial of use of all of, or part of the main computer system.

COUNTERMEASURE:

The employment of devices, measures or techniques having as their objective the removal or reduction of threats.

DATA CUSTODIAN:

The person(s) who is responsible for the accuracy of authorised data updates/creation/deletion.

DATA INTEGRITY:

The property that data has not been altered or destroyed in an unauthorised manner.

DATA OWNER:

The person within an organisation who has ultimate responsibility for the accuracy and integrity of a data file.

DATA SECURITY:

The protection of data from accidental, unauthorised, intentional or malicious modification, destruction or disclosure.

ENCRYPTION ALGORITHM:

A set of mathematically expressed rules for rendering information unintelligible by effecting a series of transformations to the normal representation of the information through the use of variable elements controlled by the application of a key.

INTEGRITY:

See Data Integrity.

KEY:

A sequence of symbols that controls the operations of encipherment and decipherment.

KEY MANAGEMENT: The generation, storage, secure distribution and application of keys in accordance with a security policy.

LIFE CYCLE: All stages during the life of a system from initial User Requirements specification through implementation until the system ceases to be operational.

LOGIC BOMB: A section of code (in a program) that can be triggered to run at a later date (the date is often the trigger).

PASSWORD: A protected word or string of characters that identifies or authenticates a user, a specific resource, or an access type.

PHYSICAL SECURITY: The measures used to provide physical protection of resources against deliberate and accidental threats.

RECOVERY: The preparation and execution of plans for the restoration subsequent to a disaster situation, of the normal mode of operation.

RECOVERY PROCEDURES: The actions necessary to restore a systems computerised capability and data files after a system failure or penetration.

REMOTE TERMINALS: Terminals and peripheral devices which are located outside the central computer facility.

RISK: The probability or likelihood that a threat against a system, facility or operation could successfully cause loss of integrity, availability or confidentiality of the system facility or operation.

RISK ANALYSIS: An analysis of system assets and vulnerabilities to establish an expected loss from certain events based on estimated probabilities of occurrence of those events.

RISK ASSESSMENT: The process of evaluating threats and vulnerabilities both known and postulated, to determine expected loss and establish the degree of acceptability to system operators.

RISK MANAGEMENT: An element of managerial science concerned with the identification, measurement, control and minimisation of uncertain events.

SAFEGUARDS: See Countermeasure.

SALAMI TECHNIQUE: "Slicing off" small amounts from individual financial records, accumulating the small amounts and transferring the total to an unauthorised account (often, "rounding-down" remainders are used).

**SERVICE LEVEL
AGREEMENT (SLA):**   An agreed level of service required by the user in the event of disaster causing total or partial disruption of the computer system.

SECURITY: Minimising the risk of exposure of assets and resources to various vulnerabilities.

SOFTWARE INTEGRITY: See Data Integrity.

STANDBY: See Back Up

SYSTEM LIFE CYCLE: See Life Cycle

TAPPING,
WIRETAPPING   A: Active. The attaching of an unauthorised device,
                   such as a computer terminal, to a communica-
                   tions circuit, for the purpose of obtaining ac-
                   cess to data through the generation of false mes-
                   sages or control signals, or by altering the com-
                   munication of legitimate users.

                   B: Passive. The monitoring and/or recording of
                   data while the data is being transmitted over a
                   communications link.

THREAT: A potential violation of security.

THREAT AGENT: Those methods and things (e.g. fire, natural dis-
                   aster, etc.) which may exploit a vulnerability in a
                   DP system, facility or operation.

TROJAN HORSE: An entity which, when introduced to the sys-
                   tem, has an unauthorised effect in addition to
                   its authorised function.

USER-ID: User Identification - a non-secret code by
                   which the user is known to the computer system.

VULNERABILITY: Any weakness or flaw existing in an automated
                   system or its environment.

ANNEX C

PASSWORDS

The password has been regarded as a significant element of computer security for a considerable period. It has also been regarded as one of the weakest points in the security of systems. The reason for its longevity is that the password represents the most cost-effective alternative to other current methods of controlling access to computer systems.

The most common password weaknesses encountered are:

* Users forget passwords
* Users write them down and leave them near terminals
* Group passwords become well-known outside the group
* Passwords are not always encrypted when stored on disk
* Passwords are not changed often enough (if at all)
* Password changes are difficult to enforce
* Users alternate between two passwords
* If password changes are enforced, users may change on one day, than change back to their usual password on the following day.

Content of Password

Passwords should be kept secret. The more people who know, or who can guess, the password, the less secret it will be. Avoid choosing passwords with which you can be easily associated. Examples include the names of spouses and children, car registration marks and telephone numbers etc. Where possible do not choose a combination of keys which can easily be interpreted as it is typed (AAAA, ASDF, etc). Research has shown that in each country a very small number of words are used by a large number of users as passwords. For example, in The Netherlands "GEHEIM" is the most popular password - in the UK "SECRET" is.

When the range of characters for use in a password is given as the full range of ASCII printable characters (i.e 96 characters) a three character password would have a theoretical maximum number of combinations of 96 X 96 X 96, approximately 885,000.

In reality, few people will use numbers or punctuation marks or differentiate between upper and lower case letters, which reduces the theoretical maximum to something closer to 26 X 26 X 26, and, of these, most three letter words will have a vowel in the middle position which further reduces the maximum to 26 X 5 X 26, approximately 3400. By exhaustive testing of all combinations even a slow human operator could probably manage to crack the system in a few days. A determined hacker could manage to do so using his micro-computer in a very short time.

One way of reducing the choice of likely passwords is to disallow the use of vowels which would exclude many obvious passwords. Another may be to insist that a punctuation mark is used somewhere in the password.

Research is being carried out in the area of system generated random passwords and user generated passwords to determine respectively a realistically useable subset and a realistically excludeable subset. System generated random patterns of characters tend to be difficult to remember so users write them down - with immediate compromise. The research is to limit the randomness to produce near-words which will be more acceptable. Similarly password "editors" are examining passwords at installations to determine a set of disallowable words - like SECRET etc.

Other related areas of password security include double passwords for users, where the user must enter two passwords before access is permitted, and half-passwords, where two users each enter half of one password.

The former method could be enhanced by having one system generated password and one user generated password which is more likely to produce unrelated passwords, or by restricting users to (e.g.) alphabetic keys in one password and numeric keys in the second.

Half-passwords could be used to protect particularly sensitive transactions which the organisation security policy has dictated must be carried out under supervision. The person who is to perform the transaction enters, say, the first four characters of the password, while the supervisor enters the last four characters. The security relies on the assumption that the user and the supervisor do not communicate their half of the password to each other. Both personnel must be present before the transaction can be initiated.

Length of Password

Some systems specify a minimum length, some a maximum length and some both. Some allow the system manager to alter the minimum and maximum to suit local requirements. A greater degree of protection is offered on longer passwords. Fixed length passwords (i.e the same minimum and maximum) afford the greatest opportunity for automatic guessing which might be carried out by another computer dialing in and simply working its way through the list of allowable passwords. A range of five to twelve characters would probably be acceptable.

Longer passwords, also unknown as pass-phrases, may allow the user a greater choice of passwords including misspellings and incorrect punctuation. Users may also select short pharases from a foreign language.

In the case of short passwords, users could select acronyms derived from phrases. For example, "FFTTO" could represent "Five, Four, Three, Two, One".

Life of Password

The more exposure a password has, through either its frequency of use or its longevity, the greater the chance of possible compromise. Passwords may also be compromised while in use, during transmission and during storage. Passwords may be known to several people and are often stored in text files which are not protected to the same degree that a password ought to be.

A user's password should be changed or deleted if the user:

* **terminates employment (resignation or dismissal);**
* **transfers to another position which does not require access;**
* **is undergoing disciplinary action.**

There may also be a requirement to review the passwords of other system users if any of the above circumstances arise.

Password changes should be governed by a password's maximum lifetime. The purpose of this is to encourage users to change their passwords regularly, for example, on a monthly basis. Some security systems force all users to change their passwords during the first working day of the month, others will permit users to change their passwords at a time convenient to themselves.

The former approach could place a temporary instantaneous load on the security software, while the latter requires that the security system stores, and maintains, the expiry date of each user's password.

Passwords changes may also be governed by a minimum lifetime, the purpose of which is to prevent users from changing passwords, and then immediately changing back to the previous password. It should be possible to override the minimum lifetime in some circumstances, particularly in the case of a suspected compromise to password security. When users enter the necessary dialogue to change their passwords, the system should re-authenticate the user by requesting the user's current password. This process guards against the possibility that an unauthorised user changes the password of an authorised user while the latter is temporarily distracted by, for example, a telephone call.

Also, the password change dialogue should verify the user's new password by requesting that it is entered twice to guard against the possibility that it is inadvertently mistyped.

There may be a requirement for one-off passwords. For instance an authorised user using the system for the first time needs to be assigned a one-off password which he must immediately change when he signs on to the system. Similarly a user who rarely uses the system may forget his password (just as we all occasionally forget telephone numbers) and so a one-off password could be used to permit him to sign on. The responsibility for creating one-off passwords should rest with the individual with overall responsibility for security management.

Other uses of one-off passwords (and user-ids) include system troubleshooting. In emergency circumstances, a person who does not normally have access to the system is temporarily granted access to perform an agreed emergency function. All one-off passwords (and user-ids) should have a lifetime considerably shorter than that of ordinary passwords.

Accountability

All users should be responsible for the secrecy of their passwords and responsible, therefore, for all activity carried out on the system and attributable to their own user-id/password combination.

Group passwords should be avoided where possible because this individual accountability is compromised.

Password Communication

Some Access Control systems require that there is a system manager responsible for maintenance of the list of authorised users and their permissions etc. The system manager may also be responsible for the creation of one-off passwords and communicating them to the individual users. The most secure method of informing users of their passwords is "face-to-face", although an alternative is delivery in a sealed envelope by trusted courier. Note that the user-id and password should never be communicated together, just as banks send cash-cards and PIN's (Personal Identity Numbers) under separate cover.

Password Storage, Access and Encryption

Passwords have to be stored on the system, and because the security system must have access to the passwords, so might an unauthorised person. The password file should therefore be protected in such a way that only the security (or related) software can access it. Where this is not possible the passwords should be encrypted or coded in some manner that ensures that only the appropriate software can understand them.

Password Entry and Non-display

Passwords can be vulnerable to being read by people other than the user, during entry to the system. On screen devices the display attributes of the terminal should be used by the security system to hide the input as it is entered. On hard-copy devices the transmission should be switched to half duplex (no echo) or each character of the password should be overprinted with other characters to ensure that the password is not legible. Users should ensure that others cannot see the keyboard while they are entering their password.

To allow for inadvertent typing errors, users should have at least two attempts to enter a correct password, but not, of course an infinite number which would permit exhaustive password searching. The number of attempts should be determined by the possibilities for action on failure. Ideally, on failure, the user should be given no guidance, other than the fact that an error has been made, i.e. no indication should be given that the user entered a wrong user-id or a wrong password.

Even less should the user-id or password be dynamically verified (character by character) with entry of excluded characters (e.g vowels) disallowed automatically. Users should only have a short time (approximately one minute) to enter their user-id and password before the system disables (times out) the terminal. Generally the third successive failure to enter a correct user-id/password combination should invoke appropriate security action. This should include logging to a violation file that an invalid sign-on attempt has been made.

Further security action could include disabling the terminal for a random or predetermined time period and/or alerting the security manager that an attempted breach has occurred. In the case of single-user and some multi-user systems (including personal computers shared by a number of users) these facilities may not be available. In the case when the access control system is implemented as an add-on board all its security files should be stored in battery protected memory (not disk) to ensure that their status is continuous - even across a power failure.

Password Transmission

When accessing a network, user-ids and passwords are sometimes transmitted from the point of entry to the point of verification (the system). To minimise the chance of disclosure the host may immediately encrypt the password prior to verification. There remains, however, the chance that the password is compromised during transmission. Two possibilities exist to reduce this chance. First the password verification may take place at the point of entry, in which case the password is not transmitted. The second possibility is that the password is encrypted prior to its transmission to the host where it is decrypted and verified.

Authentication Period

Once a user has been authenticated by the system, the system makes the reasonable assumption that the same user remains until initiating a disconnect or signing off. A period of keyboard inactivity (i.e. no user input) or screen inactivity (no system output) could indicate that the user has become distracted (e.g. answering the telephone) or has left the vicinity of the terminal. An implementation of a typical "clear desk" policy on the computer system is to force a disconnection after a short period of inactivity.

This time-out period should vary according to the user's access rights or the activity that was being performed: if the user is the system's master user then the period should be shorter than it would be for others. Generally a period of about 5 minutes will be sufficient. The user, on return, will have to go through the process of signing on again to re-authenticate. Some access control systems record the fact that the user has been timed out as a security violation. When he signs on again the system may ask for an explanation from the user, which together with the date and time will appear on the security manager's regular security violation report. The security manager may then instigate further investigation.

Immediately prior to changing his password the user should have to re-authenticate.

Session Passwords

In a highly secure environment, a user may be required to re-authenticate himself at regular intervals (every ten minutes, say) or at specific points when invoking sensitive programs or accessing sensitive files. Also a user may be given a temporary password during the sign-on process for use in response to random request for re-authentication. This password operates more like a "codeword of the day" rather than a password. In an ideal situation users should have to re-authenticate themselves with a new password each time but it would place too great a burden on users to choose and remember a new password every few minutes.

Pass Algorithms

Another form of user authentication is the pass-algorithm in which the user remembers a method of deriving a password. The user enters a user-id as normal, and the system responds with a message, such as:

" The pass-algorithm must be kept secret " .

The user has previously been told that the pass-algorithm or method to derive the password is to respond with "every third letter of the message (excluding spaces and punctuation)" and therefore responds:

"ESLRHUBESR"

(i.e. "thE paSs-aLgoRitHm mUst Be kEpt SecRet"

The next user to sign on will, of course, be presented with a different message, but will use the same pass-algorithm to derive a password. A library of phrases must be maintained, and these changed regularly. The pass-algorithm relies on secrecy of the user-id to maintain individual accountability but otherwise operates in a manner similar to group passwords.

Forced Password Change

Two systems of forced password change may be implemented. In the first, the user is reminded at sign-on that a password change is due, and requested to change password during the signed-on session. The second form actually engages the user in the necessary dialogue to change password before performing any normal processing.

In either case there may be a form of graceful degradation in which the user's facilities are reduced as the password change becomes more and more overdue. Typically a "warning" is generated at 30 days overdue from an exception report, at 45 days the security manager will inform the user's manager and at 60 days the user will be deemed to no longer require access and the user-id and password will be removed from the system. In any of these cases the degree of automation of these facilities will vary and the thresholds of 30, 45 and 60 days will be variable, depending on the system selected and the security requirements of the system.

ANNEX D

OTHER ACCESS CONTROL METHODS

Any identification and verification system must rely on uniqueness or secrecy. Passwords are the most common form of verification, however some systems make use of more sophisticated techniques.

Identification and verification of identity require two pieces of information usually selected from the following:

* **Something you know, for example, user-id, password**
* **Something you hold, for example, a magnetic card or a key**
* **Something you are, for example, signature, fingerprints**

The typical user-id/password combination (something known/something known) is weak in comparison to a typical physical access implementation in which a turnstile requires the use of a magnetic card (something held) and a digital code (something known).

With this in mind, a great deal of research is being done on more secure user identification and verification methods.

Amongst these methods, the most important ones are:

* **Tokens**
* **Handheld password generators**
* **Biometric Access Controls**

Tokens

Tokens fall into two categories, dumb and intelligent. Dumb tokens include ordinary keys at the low end and magnetic stripe cards at the higher end.

Intelligent tokens are personified by the smart card, which has a microprocessor and memory. Other forms include handheld password generators which are discussed later.

Tokens are rarely used in the small or medium-sized computer system environment. However, some equipment manufacturers are performing research in this field and there are products available.

Smart Cards

Most computer system manufacturers, and many large users are focussing their development and attention on smart cards.

Smart cards are similar in form to credit cards, but differ from magnetic stripe cards in that the card has a microprocessor embedded in the card with some memory, which thus gives the card some intelligence. The memory is usually divided into secure and non-secure, where the difference is that the former can only be accessed by the card's own processor while the latter can also be accessed by the external processor (such as the card-reader). The card's secure area could be used for storing the holder's identification details, access rights and other similar data.

Magnetic Stripe Cards

This is one of the most common forms of token, and in the most convenient form looks like a credit card. The card uses a conventional tape-like recording process on one, two or three parallel tracks which run the length of the magnetic stripe. There are international standards for the recording process. This type of card is frequently used in banking applications with a personal number password for cash withdrawals at automated teller machines (ATMs). Because the technology is well known, there is a threat of counterfeiting.

Some manufacturers of these cards have embedded a unique code into the stripe which can only be interpreted by special equipment and cannot be altered or erased. Other developments, such as high coercivity tape, have also helped to reduce the threat of counterfeiting.

Hollerith Cards

These have a series of holes punched in them which uniquely identify the holder. Holes can easily be covered up and new holes added, which can compromise their security.

Embossed Cards

These are similar to Hollerith cards and contain a pattern raised from the surface. Like the Hollerith card, the pattern can be altered and is visible to the naked eye.

Bar Codes

These frequently appear on photocards used for visual identification and are machine readable. The machine readibility is most often exploited for physical access control with the holder's photograph providing visual authentication. The bar code may be visible or invisible to the naked eye depending on the type of reader preferred (or the security requirements).

Handheld Password Generators

The objective of these devices (also called random password generators - RPGs) is to generate a one-off password as often as required in order that the user can re-authenticate at the request of the security system.

Typically, the system will go through the process of requesting a user-id from the user followed by displaying a "challenge" which the user will input to the hand-held device which will then generate a "response". The user then enters the "response" to the system which authenticates the user's right to use the system. In some cases, the user must authenticate himself to the password generator, while in others, the "challenge" is a random pattern of dots on an area of the screen which are interpreted by photo-electric cells on the password generator, which then generates a password.

Biometric Access Controls

Biometrics use fundamental attributes of the individual to identify and verify him. These attributes include:-

* fingerprints
* hand geometry
* retinal eyescan
* signature dynamics
* voice patterns

Not all of these are relevant as logical access controls but research is being carried out in all of the above areas for physical access controls. These controls are not in general use, but may be applicable for particularly sensitive systems.

There is a general opinion that the first three above would not currently be widely socially acceptable. Fingerprinting, for example, is associated with suspected criminals. Automatic signature checking is the most acceptable biometric check.

Biometric research and development recognises two classic errors, Type I and Type II. A Type I error is the rejection of a valid person (also known as the insult rate), while a Type II error is the acceptance of an invalid person.

The occurrence rates of the two types of error are inversely related in that as the accuracy of the acceptance parameters are tightly constrained - to prevent an invalid acceptance - there is a greater likelihood that a genuine identity claim will be rejected. Similarly, if the parameters are not tightly constrained - to prevent a valid identity claim from being rejected - there is a greater probability that an invalid claim will be accepted.

When a new person is introduced to a biometric access control system he is enrolled by providing a sample or samples of the relevant data. In the case of signatures, the normal practice is to record at least two signatures, and from these extract the relevant parameters which will be measured. These parameters can be statistically analysed to allow for slight differences in the signature, and so the statistical average signature is stored, together with expected variations in the parameters. Over a period of time this data can be finely tuned with the new data which is available whenever the person signs in.

Another possibility at enrollment is to record for example, the signature parameters, in the magnetic stripe of a card, or in the memory of a smart card. The user carries the token (something you hold) and uses this to declare himself to a card reader which also functions as a signature verifier. The user authenticates his signature parameters stored in the card. There may also be a password (something you know) used in this process.

Authentication Time

All biometric access controls require more user intervention than a straightforward user- id/password combination. In addition, the time taken to authenticate can be longer. Periods of several seconds are not uncommon.

Signature Dynamics

Signature recognition is regarded as the most socially acceptable of biometric controls. Early signature verification systems examined only the physical pattern of the signature. More recent processes register the number of times the pen touched the surface, the amount of time the pen spends in the air between contacts with the surface, the pen's acceleration and deceleration, and the time it takes to complete the signature. Most people are not aware of how often they raise the pen from the paper, or how long they pause between certain portions of their signature. The old systems used a sensitive pen whereas the tendency nowadays is to use a sensitive writing pad.

In contrast to the other biometric systems, signature dynamics are not being researched with a view to physical access controls. Its social acceptability and long history as an authentication mechanism highlight it as an ideal tool for logical access control systems.

ANNEX E

ENCRYPTION AND AUTHENTICATION

Encryption is the process of transforming information (cleartext) into an unintelligible form (ciphertext) so that it may be sent over insecure channels. The transformation process is controlled by a data string (key). Anyone intercepting the ciphertext while it is in the insecure channel should require the appropriate key to decrypt (convert back to cleartext) the information. The intended receiver is assumed to have that key.

Encryption not only provides protection against unauthorised disclosure. It can also ensure the detection of unauthorised modifications of information, since any change to encrypted data (without the necessary key) will prevent successful decryption by the intended recipient. It should be clear, however, that encryption does nothing to *prevent* modification, or destruction; it simply ensures the *detection* of such events. Critical data, therefore, cannot be protected simply by encrypting it.

Although the primary application of encryption is in data communications, it has important applications in small computer environments. In effect, personal computers and their storage media can be considered "insecure channels" because of their physical accessibility.

General Cryptographic Facilities

There are several commercially available software and hardware based products which provide personal computer users with cryptographic capabilities. These products, in general, enable the user to perform the following cryptographic functions:

* enter or change cryptographic keys
* encrypt a block of data
* decrypt a block of data

In some cases, facilities are provided for the generation and management of keys. Normally, however, this is left to the user. Indeed, this can be one of the major problems in the effective use of encryption since the randomness and secrecy of keys are critical to the protection provided by cryptography.

Bulk File Encryption

The normal manner in which cryptography is used in a small computer environment is to encrypt and decrypt entire files. Typically, a user prepares a file (presumably containing sensitive information) and then runs an encryption utility to produce a ciphertext version of the file. The original file should then be overwritten. Before using the file again, the utility program must again be used to decrypt and produce a cleartext version of the file. The user is usually responsible for selecting, entering and remembering the key used for the encryption and decryption process. Commercial cryptographic products usually provide utility programs for bulk file encryption and decryption as well as a utility to overwrite old files.

Integral File Encryption

Problems with bulk encryption and decryption of data files include general inconvenience, the need to erase cleartext files, and the personnel training necessary. An alternative for file encryption is to use a cryptographic facility which is integral to the file input/output subsystem. Basically, each block of data to be written to disk is first encrypted, and each block read from disk is decrypted before it is passed to the requesting program. This makes the entire cryptographic process almost transparent to the user and eliminates the inconvenience and dangers associated with bulk file procedures. Users with sufficient technical expertise can implement such a capability themselves. In addition, there are commercial hardware and software products which may be considered.

Selection Considerations

In selecting cryptographic products, three basic considerations are important:

*   **private versus public key systems**
*   **cryptographic algorithm**
*   **hardware versus software implementation**

Private Versus Public Key Systems

There are two basic types of cryptographic systems in common use. A "private key" system requires that the sending and receiving parties share a common cryptographic key. This key must be kept secret (private) to ensure the security of the encrypted information.

This requires special precautions and protocols for the distribution of keys. Indeed, this has long been one of the difficulties in the widespread application of cryptography to large communications networks. In situations involving small numbers of users, this is generally not a significant problem, however.

A "public key" cryptosystem involves pairs of keys, one for encrypting messages and another for decrypting. The encrypting key is public, so that anyone wishing to send a message to a given user can use that person's encrypting key. Only the recipient, however, has the (secret) decryption keys This type of cryptosystem can reduce certain key management problems and can be attractive for large networks of interconnected users.

Cryptography Algorithms

All cryptosystems require a well-defined process (algorithm) by which information is transformed from cleartext to ciphertext and back to cleartext. It is an accepted principle in cryptography (the design and analysis of codes and ciphers) that the strength of a system should *not* be dependent on the secrecy of the algorithm itself. This enables the exchange of information necessary for design and manufacture of systems incorporating the algorithm. It also permits critical analysis of the algorithm itself and eliminates the need to provide physical protection for devices and documentation.

The Data Encryption Standard (DES) is currently the cryptographic standard for non-classified U.S. Federal Government applications. The DES is a private key cryptosystem and is described in Federal Information Processing Standards Publication 46 (FIPS46). It is important to note that Federal Government agencies are, in general, required to use the DES for cryptographic applications involving non- classified information.

Although there is no standard public key cryptosystem, there are algorithms that have been published in the open literature. Like the DES, they also have received considerable critical review, and the level of protection provided is relatively well understood. Several commercially available cryptographic products incorporate either the DES or the openly-available public key algorithms.

A number of commercial cryptographic products (both private and public key systems) use proprietary (secret) cryptographic algorithms. Such algorithms are often designed to operate at higher speeds than algorithms like the DES. However, since the algorithms are not made public, it is difficult to obtain an objective evaluation of their cryptographic strength.

Hardware Versus Software

Cryptographic algorithms can, in general, be implemented in either hardware or software. The former approach usually results in much faster operation and better integrity protection while the latter approach is often cheaper and more flexible. Hardware implementations of the DES on a single integrated circuit chip are available and are used in a number of cryptographic products. Full compliance with the DES requires hardware implementation, although software versions of the DES algorithm are available.

Authentication

As mentioned above, encryption will offer protection against disclosure. Authentication is a similar technique which offers a means of detecting modification. Authentication uses a key and algorithm to derive an authentication code which is appended to the data. A subsequent user of the data can re-authenticate the data using the same key and algorithm to verify that the data has not been altered since the authentication code was appended. No encryption of the data has taken place and the data is therefore unprotected against disclosure. Also, authentication does not protect against modification but merely provides a means of detecting it.

As with encryption, authentication relies on the secrecy of the key. Data can be authenticated at various levels, such as a single message on a network, or a file on a disk. As software programs may be regarded as data files, authentication may provide a mechanism for detecting modification to software.

The data can, of course, be encrypted and then authenticated to protect against disclosure and to detect modification.

Key Management

A major part of any encryption/authentication system is key management. The key is the vehicle used to encrypt and decrypt files - users must therefore take care to protect their keys. If a key is lost, stolen or disclosed, the system's security is severely compromised.

The term "key management" refers to the secure generation, distribution and storage of encryption keys. The keys should be generated in a random fashion to make it extremely unlikely that anyone could guess the individual keys or discover the method of generation.

Encryption algorithms generally permit longer keys than password systems do. (The encryption key can be regarded as a type of password.) Full use of the key length should be made. Some systems allow the user to select a long key which is compressed to a shorter encryption key which is used directly by the encryption algorithm. The encryption key can, of course, be used directly with the short key if it is selected. However the advantage of using a long key and having it compressed is that the derived short key is unlikely to be easily guessable (to allow unauthorised decryption) and will use the characters (such as punctuation marks etc.) which are outside the normal range of selection which a human operator would choose.

ANNEX F

SURVIVAL PLAN CONTENTS

1. **INTRODUCTION**
   How to use the Survival Plan
   Survival Plan Synopsis
   Policy Statement
   Project Objectives
   Distribution List

2. **DUTIES OF THE SURVIVAL COORDINATOR**
   Overview and Summary
   Survival Training Program
   Training Schedule
   Testing Program
   Disaster Drill Testing
   Maintenance Procedures
   Maintenance Responsibilities
   Functions During Recovery Effort
   Plan Activation
   Establishing a Control Centre

3. **SURVIVAL TASKS**
   Recovery Strategies
   Recovery Procedure
   Task Assignments/Responsibilities
   Task Procedures
   Organisation Chart
   Priority Definitions
   Application Priorities
   Control Centre Location
   Critical Services

Contact Lists for: - Alternate Systems
                                    - Users
                                    - Staff

Vendors and Servicers of: - Hardware
                                    - Telecommunications
                                    - Software
                                    - Manuals
                                    - Off-Site Storage Facilities

Inventory Lists for: - Forms and Supplies
                                    - Manuals
                                    - Software

Procedures for: - Power Up
                                    - Power Down
                                    - Back-up/Restore
                                    - Online Network
                                    - Report and Fiche Distribution
                                    - Storage
                                    - Retention
                                    - Keying/Data Entry
                                    - Systems Software Restoration
                                    - Data Base Restoration
                                    - Application Reload/Restart
                                    - Physical Security
                                    - Data Security

4. APPENDICES

Building Specifications
Network Configuration
Cabling Diagrams(s)
Building Blueprints
Control Centre Requirements

ANNEX G

INDEX